Prologue

LILLY LUMBERS PEACEFULLY ahead of me along the narrow mountain trail. Left and right, she rips off grass and branches with her trunk and, curling this up, feeds them into her mouth where she slowly grinds them down into something that will eventually be dumped at my feet as a big light-brown ball, the stems still visible.

The monsoon has made the steep muddy paths hard going, but the small troop of elephants climbs stoically uphill. Lilly spots a banana tree on the left, below the path. Undaunted by the steep slope, she lowers her 6,500 pounds, wraps her trunk caressingly around the stem, and plucks it from the ground as if it were a dandelion.

Up and up we go. Rice fields and plantations are now giving way to shrubs and denser stretches of beautiful deciduous forest, though there are hardly any big trees left. We pass a stream below a waterfall. After the animals have drunk their fill, they climb the slope up towards the house raised on stilts where we will sleep tonight. We are in Elephant Haven.

We stretch out on the wooden veranda in front of the tiny bedrooms. The elephants take off towards freedom, ears flapping, and trunks high. Every now and then, we hear their awe-inspiring rumble, a prehistoric sound, sometimes followed by exuberant trumpeting. We gaze out over the forest through pouring rain. Sometimes we hear the distant drone of chainsaws. Logging is illegal but still continues.

At nightfall, we build a fire; the air cools quickly up here in the mountains of northern Thailand. The mahouts play games, we drink beer. Nothing beats a beer after a tropically warm day. Pom and I start talking. Pom is a pillar of the Elephant Nature Park; she can read elephants like a book. She can also cook a five-star meal on a charcoal fire and turn herbs and leaves into medicine. She is petite, as Thai ladies often are, but she drinks and smokes like a lord. One night, while she and I were driving to the Park, she suddenly braked. 'Cobra!' A long dark shadow slithered over the path in front of us and into the verge.

Pom leant out of the window and told the snake a story that lasted for minutes. She's got a thing about cobras.

We're comfortable near the campfire and can't stop talking. I would so much like to do more than simply be a volunteer in the Elephant Nature Park for just a few weeks every year. The Park is wonderful but it's too small. It can't take care of all the elephants in distress. So many trudge the city streets, begging, together with their mahouts. So many get exhausted and injured while carrying tourists around on their backs in trekking camps. The world needs a wake-up call. What can I do?

That night the plan was born. If Mark Shand could do it, I can too! He bought an elephant and travelled with it through India. The book he wrote about the trip kept me up for nights. What if I bought two street elephants in Bangkok and walked with them right through Thailand's countryside to the Elephant Nature Park? It would cause a stir, and a stir was exactly what was needed. Before the dust settled, one could draw attention to the fate of street elephants, plead for more living space, for ecotourism. Pom is excited. 'Good plan, Antoinette! Maybe the Park can provide people to help you. You will need mahouts, a vet, and a manager to take care of the permits. You will also need a pick-up truck for the luggage and for the elephant food. You can't just assume they will find enough fodder on the road, so you need to count on four hundred pounds per elephant per day.' Always the practical one, Pom. Suddenly a total price tag looms through the campfire smoke plumes. How much would an elephant cost? And a pick-up truck? And all those people who will also have to eat? But I am no longer to be stopped. After all, aren't I a professional fundraiser? I'll just go and find the money in the Netherlands. And we'll call the project *Bring the elephant home*.

The Great Elephant Escape

Antoinette van de Water

Liesbeth Sluiter

Translated by

Joy Carolus and Janette Symons

SILKWORM BOOKS

ISBN: 978-974-9511-64-0

First published in Dutch in 2006 by
Uitgeverij BZZTôH bv, 's-Gravenhage, The Netherlands

Published in 2009 by
Silkworm Books
6 Sukkasem Road, T. Suthep
Chiang Mai 50200, Thailand
info@silkwormbooks.com
http://www.silkwormbooks.com

Typeset by Silk Type in Minion Pro 10 pt.
Cover photograph by Julia S. Ferdinand
Printed and bound in Thailand by Printing House, Bangkok

10 9 8 7 6 5 4 3 2 1

Contents

1

Introducing the Cast

I DREW UP MY first business plan when I was seven years old. I wanted a dog but my parents didn't quite trust me. They saw themselves suffering the fate of all those other parents who fall for their children's pleas: walking the dog and scooping its poop. But this didn't throw me off track. I made a timetable for walking the dog and a plan of how I'd take care of it. I asked around about the price of a dog, and the price of a basket, food, and a leash. There was a big difference in price between a basket and a crate. I made a budget. When I had saved up enough money from birthdays and car washing, I bought Moppie. Moppie and I became one. I had her wear clothes and taught her tricks. One winter when she ended up in a ditch because she thought she could walk on duckweed, I jumped into the water, pulled her out and made her wear my jacket. She slept in my bed and went to school with me, and even once to the College of Economics.

Economics is a useful study. I learned more about business plans, and discovered how to build up something from nothing. I was given the tools to realise dreams. After graduation, I got an office job in a business company where I became utterly miserable. It was obvious I was on the wrong track. I didn't want to have anything to do with money anymore and started thinking about what was really important to me: animals and the environment. I made a 180-degree turn. Within a year I had swapped my commercial job, my boyfriend, my semi-detached house, and fast car for a job with the Dutch branch of Friends of the Earth, a part-time course in anthropology, a girlfriend, shared living in an old school, and a bicycle. 'Can't you ever take it easy?' my parents sighed.

At Friends of the Earth I became a fundraiser. Again to do with money, but this time to help realise things I believed in. Every euro earned made me happy and FoE felt like home. I bonded with many of my colleagues. What's more, I joined their climbing team and did fantastic stunts during campaigns, like hanging banners across skyscrapers, and dangling from a crane at Schiphol airport for fourteen hours. Believe me, it can be freezing cold on a crane and your thoughts slow down. Afterwards, I once spent an entire hour wondering whether I should eat a seitan bun or a raisin bun.

***

It may sound strange but my love for animals has a lot to do with cruelty against animals; in fact, with not being able to stand cruelty against animals. When I was a child, I saw a film about a fox in a trap that gnawed off its own leg in order to escape. For years, I couldn't get that image out of my mind. What would I have done in that situation? Once in a while, I still also dream about the time my father took me to a slaughterhouse. When he later showed me a pan of meat and told me where it had come from, I decided I would never eat animals again. My first real attempt at vegetarianism was later, though, after a school film about the bio-industry. But it didn't last long, even then.

Our home was a hospital for all the sick and barely alive birds I found. To my unimaginable horror, Moppie once bit one to death. My spider aquarium had to go when one night the pair of tights I had stretched over it came off, and I found all the spiders were running around loose. The flies' graveyard in a matchbox on the window ledge lasted longer.

I connect easily with animals. There's a feeling of trust between us. Animals are pure. Without them life wouldn't be the same. When I see how elephants take care of each other, I feel happy inside.

That's why it was no surprise that I ended up in the Elephant Nature Park in 2002 when I was on holiday in Asia, looking for a place where I could make myself useful. I was twenty-seven and travelling alone for the first time. I figured I had to discover myself. I quickly get bored lying on the beach or travelling around. I prefer to contribute to society and get to know people as equals.

There was an endless number of volunteer programmes in Asia. 'It's not a matter of searching but of finding,' a friend had told me. The first project I seriously considered was the Elephant Nature Park. A nature reserve for elephants that have been traumatised by being forced to beg on the streets or from being worked to death in trekking camps. Within two weeks, I was on an airplane to Thailand with a strange feeling in my stomach.

The first night I was in Bangkok, I started partying right off. On Khaosan Road, a nightlife hub of the city, it's not difficult to get in touch with other travellers. Throughout the warm night, the beer flowed lavishly, as did wild plans and stories about exotic adventures. Until, completely unexpectedly, I came face to face with an elephant. He was wandering around in the middle of the night, traffic rushing by on all sides, his body covered with wounds and infections. He could stand on his hind legs and bow, and his mahout collected the money. I was shocked. When I took the night train north three days later, my motivation to help elephants had been strongly reinforced.

***

Her name is Sangduen Chailert but everyone calls her Lek, which means 'Little One' in Thai. She weighs no more than eighty pounds but everything else about her is big. She has a compelling voice and a charismatic personality. Besides a travel agency in Chiang Mai, she also runs the Elephant Nature Park. Her life is all about elephants. Listen to Lek's story.

'I grew up in a village in northern Thailand, in a family with seven children. My grandfather was a shaman, a traditional healer. One day, when he had healed the son of a tribal chief, he was given an elephant by way of thanks. I fell in love with the elephant immediately and called him Golden Treasure. We played with him. He was the mountain we could climb over and the cave we could hide in. Once, my mother had to pull my little brother out of his mouth; he had crawled in because he wanted to know what was inside. He never hurt us. *Chang* (elephants) are better at loving than we are.'

Lek's family owns a trekking camp, of which there are many in Thailand. Lek started it, took care of the construction work, and was registered as the owner. Even as a child she was horrified by the violence used to train the elephants, and by their bad working conditions. As a teenager, she roamed the forest looking for elephants working in the logging industry.

'I saw wounds with worms crawling out of them. There were many sick animals. They were given amphetamines to work longer. I travelled around with a backpack filled with medicines. I saw how an elephant was lured into an enclosure and killed by the falling gate. I saw how newly captured baby elephants were being battered to break their will. Half of these elephants die. Mothers in captivity sometimes kill their babies, and not without reason. It is worse now than thirty years ago. There used to be more respect, people used to see something magical in elephants. The bond between a mahout and his elephant was a bond for life. Today many mahouts see their work as a job like all others. While wild elephants are a protected species, tamed elephants are cattle. An owner can do as he likes with them. Tamed elephants should be protected by law as well.'

Lek never disguises her feelings. When she started to criticise the trekking industry and the training of elephants, her family was not amused. Every day they fought. After one of those clashes, in which Lek's father called her the black sheep of the family, her brother convinced her father to change the ownership papers. Together they kicked Lek out. 'I forgive you, but this is the last day I call you "father"', were Lek's parting words. She left the family camp with five elephants and entered the jungle. On a mountainside she started Elephant Haven. The area belonged to the government who gave her permission to use it. She built a hut with a kitchen, a porch, three tiny rooms, and a toilet cubicle with a hole in the ground. She got the mahouts of the five elephants to stay there. Not long after, the first volunteers arrived through her travel agency. Meanwhile, her backpack with medicines had grown into the Jumbo Express. With a jeep and mainly foreign volunteers, Lek visited villages to treat sick elephants in the trekking business and in villages.

Her father and some of her siblings thought she had gone mad. 'This way you'll never get rich,' they said. Lek didn't care. 'Elephants are supposed to live in the wild,' she said, 'but as long as there are tame elephants, they should be given what they are entitled to: a natural habitat, love, and respect.'

***

The Thai are extremely sensitive to criticism about their country. A frontal attack is unheard of. It is considered a crime and can even alienate your allies, and reflect negatively upon yourself. Lek stamps like a bull through this china shop.

Several years ago, in a village near the Thai-Burmese border, she filmed the cruelty inherent in the traditional method of training a young elephant. The means of restraint is called a *phajaan*, literally 'a crush'. To break its will, the villagers lock the elephant in a small wooden cage in which it cannot move around. They beat and poke it in the most sensitive places: its trunk, ears, and between its toes. It goes hungry and thirsty. It has to submit to the mahout who, at the same time, must become its confidant. To bring this about, the mahout talks soothingly to the elephant and rewards it for progress. Sometimes he brings it sugar cane or bananas in the night. This routine goes on until the animal gives up resisting, usually after about a week. Then the real training can begin. The elephant learns to follow specific commands. There are about forty—which just goes to show how smart a creature it is. The *phajaan* has been used for centuries, wherever elephants work for people. Maybe not always with the same level of cruelty but the wooden cage is commonly used. A booklet from the national forestry organisation published in 1999 describes this training method of locking up elephants in wooden cages or 'crushers', with their front legs bound together. In that same booklet, by the way, it says that elephants need a two-day rest after three days of work and should be given light duties when over fifty and retire at sixty. Perhaps it's more an ideal than the actual practice, but the trekking industry could learn a lot from these standards.

***

In 2002, the *phajaan* images Lek had filmed came into the hands of Peta, an international animal rights organisation. They proceeded to call for a worldwide ban on tourism in Thailand. After that, Lek was slandered and threatened in the media and beyond. She was said to be a smart, profit-seeking businesswoman with top-level connections. The biggest blow came when an underworld thug put a gun to her head and ordered her to declare on television that she had faked the *phajaan* herself. She went to the studio and described the *phajaan* in all its gory detail.

Meanwhile, she drew up her own plan. In 2002, Elephant Haven opened an annexe called The Farm, a small-scale facility to take care of baby elephants. It soon got crowded. In 2003, Lek sold her land and her house. With the proceedings, together with money from foreigner supporters and the profits from the travel agency, she bought a hundred-square acres of undeveloped land on the Mae Taeng river, about forty miles north of Chiang Mai. 'On the day we moved in, there was zero baht in my bank account,' she says. Now, three years later, there are thirty elephants, and new land is acquired on a regular basis. 'I will never call the Elephant Nature Park finished, I will always keep fighting for more space. A natural habitat for all elephants, that's what it's all about.

***

With some other volunteers I get off the night train, and straight into a jeep to drive off towards the Burmese border. We are on a Jumbo Express expedition. Along the border, there are mountain villages where the inhabitants, called the Karen, carried on their traditional way of living until well into the twentieth century. Ignored in the past, they are now a tourist attraction. In the centre of these villages are markets with jewellery, fabrics, and water pipes on sale. The travel agents' mini-vans are parked between the market stalls. Tourists get out to shop for half an hour and to take pictures of the locals in their authentic costumes. For an extra fee, you can see the 'long neck' Karen women, a traditional version of the *Extreme Makeover* television programme—nowadays only preserved for the tourists. Many tiers of close-fitting copper rings around the women's necks make these look longer. In fact, though, its an illusion created by forcing down the women's collar- and shoulder-bones.

Scattered around this border region, where commercial fantasies take precedence over mundane realities, are the elephant trekking camps. What better combination is there than a trip to a mountain village and then a ride through the jungle on the back of an elephant? The trips are advertised as 'eco tours'. *Explore unseen amazing Thailand, real adventure, nature trails!* The *chang*, or elephants, stand alongside the market, ready for the tourists. Wooden benches are hitched onto their backs in which up to four people can sit underneath a sunshade. These benches are large updated versions of the traditional howdah on which a monarch or aristocrat used to parade in isolated glory. You'd never guess but an elephant's back is not strong. It is better to sit on his powerful neck. The curved structure of the spine is fragile. It's true that an elephant can pull over two thousand pounds and lift hundreds of pounds with its trunk but it shouldn't carry more than two hundred pounds on his back. The bench weighs at least a hundred pounds, so with four passengers it adds up to a definite overload.

At the trekking camp we visit with the Jumbo Express, where we find elephants that are in a bad state. Skin irritations have developed into wounds that have become infected from lack of treatment. A female looks like she won't last much longer; her ribs are showing, her feet and back have open sores, her head and ears are covered with festering wounds from the steel hooked goad the mahout has used on her. She reacts to nothing and has a dull, sullen look in her eyes. Drugs, says Lek, to keep her working beyond exhaustion. We disinfect the wounds. Everyone is quiet. Lek and her co-workers talk to the owners of the camp. They give them information about how to handle elephants and how to take care of them. We leave medication behind. As we drive off, we see the bench going back up on her back.

***

For the next three weeks my life is full of elephants: trunks, trumpeting, tails, dung, elephant fun, and elephant misery. There are five adults living in Elephant Haven, and The Farm shelters three young ones. Jabu is three years old, Hope is one, and Gingmai is just six months. For several hours after my arrival, I am speechless. I don't know where to look. Gingmai does; he is looking at me, first from a distance and then he comes closer. His clumsy little trunk grasps my neck and softly brushes my face. Is he kissing me? I am in love! Over the next few days he keeps touching my face with his trunk. Eventually, I blow on its tip. He stops dead in his tracks and then blows back hard. He runs away, stops, looks over his shoulder, and runs back to me to try again. Just like a child, only he's an orphan. Gingmai's mother was killed by villagers to stop her from raiding their plantations. Gingmai, just a few days old, ran away and was found a little later, stuck between some tree trunks. He was practically dead. At The Farm, he was brought back to life. When Lek's mother died, Lek didn't think she would ever experience parent-child love again. But Gingmai brought back these feelings. Lek took care of him as if he were her own baby and spent day and night with him. During their walks, Lek taught him the things he could and could not eat, like a true mother elephant.

Jabu arrived not long ago. She was the baby elephant in the *phajaan* that Lek videotaped. Jabu had fought to the bitter end. Two months later, she was still ill and traumatised. She wouldn't eat and her feet were infected. Narong, her mahout, brought Jabu to The Farm. When Lek was accused of faking the film footage, Narong testified in court that the *phajaan* had been customary in his village for generations. He did not object to it personally but he believed the witch hunt against Lek to be unfair. Jabu is now starting to enjoy

9

life again thanks to all the love and care and, of course, to all the bananas and pineapples.

Hope was also found in a village. His mother had just died. The baby elephant was suffering from worms and parasites, and he was as thin as a rake. The owner didn't have the money to buy him milk and asked Lek to take care of him. When he arrived at The Farm, he immediately tried to be friends with Gingmai, who wasn't interested. Hope, on the other hand, turned down the people who approached him. After a few uneasy days and nights, Lek managed to gain his trust. After that, Gingmai also changed his mind, and the babies became inseparable.

***

Taking care of baby elephants is one of the most special things I have ever done in my life. They occupy us day and night. In the wild, a baby suckles from its mother for three years before weaning, so we need to fill a lot of bottles with baby food. We swim, walk, and play with the young elephants. They are just like teenagers: they're always fooling around, they stamp their feet when they don't get their way, they trip you up, and constantly test you to see what they can get away with. Swimming is the highlight of the day. There's a small lake about half an hour's walk from The Farm. As soon as the three young ones realise where we're going, there's no stopping them. Once there, Gingmai gets excited but is also scared. You have to stay close to hold his little trunk. He anxiously puts it up in the air and panics when a drop of water enters it. Hope, on the other hand, is wild. I like climbing up on his back and holding on to him with my arms around his neck. He tries to throw me off by diving and rolling, and by other creastive moves. After a while, even Jabu approaches the bank. At first she goes no further. Hope finds this large elephant very interesting and tries to push her into the water. He sprays water on her and rears up to place his forefeet on her back. It helps Jabu to forget her traumatic past. After three weeks, all four of us are swimming. We play the game of who can splash the others the hardest: I use my hands, Hope his head, Jabu her trunk, head, and front legs. One metric ton of elephant in frontal attack. Gingmai loses, he only has his floppy little trunk. One day, as we're walking back to The Farm after an afternoon swim, he suddenly starts screaming and franticly looking around. His trunk is bleeding and he doesn't know whether to run away or defend himself. But the monster that had sunk its teeth into him is invisible. Tired Gingmai had stepped on his own dangling trunk! Clumsiness is the most endearing part of his character. On one of our walks, we come across three little calves, who are startled to see this strange grey animal with a tail both in front and at the rear. But their reaction is nothing compared to Gingmai's. He practically jumps into my arms in panic.

***

The Farm at this stage is really nothing more than the house of Lek's sister, with a very large garden. There are bamboo huts for volunteers and mahouts, and 'bedrooms' for the baby elephants. In Gingmai's room, a sarong is hung up in such a way that he can stand underneath it, as if with a mother. In the garden, there is a small inflatable pool we fill up every day with the garden hose. Gingmai and Hope love to play in it. Of course the pool doesn't last long but then we have to come up with either a new pool or another game, like old car tires suspended from ropes, a mud pool, a ball, or tree trunks with branches the animals rub against. Their favourite game is pushing things over, like a new bamboo hut that is not entirely solid, or the kitchen. The kitchen is no more than a hut with a continuously running tap, some crates to put the dishes on, a spot for the cooking fire, and a place to put the elephant food. Gingmai's bedroom is next to the kitchen. Because of the tempting aroma of food and the muddy mess near the tap, it is an interesting place, and one day Gingmai decides to step right through the wall of his bedroom into the kitchen. The Farm is a pig-sty! Mud, elephant dung, and only the garden hose for washing. The babies turn everything into a mud bath. There's water everywhere, so it's just a matter of kicking up some dirt and rolling about in it.

One day, Lek arrives with a litter of puppies, found abandoned in a box at the market, skinny, covered with fleas, and yelping loudly. A few days later, she found five ducks left with their legs bound together, at the same market. They get to stay, too.

After four days at The Farm, I take off for Elephant Haven with Pom, five elephants, and a few volunteers. Along the way, we tie lengths of orange ribbons, blessed by Buddhist monks, to the trees. Even illegal loggers respect those. At Elephant Haven, we are camping out in the wild. We wash the elephants with water from the creek in the morning, and we give them their medication.

During the day, they usually stay close to the hut, but at night they roam in the woods. There is a banana plantation quite far from the hut. The elephants can't manage the distance there and back in one night, so the mahouts usually track them down again in the morning. Then, one night, Lilly contrives to disappear. All the elephants wear wooden bells with their own sound but hers is nowhere to be heard. It wasn't until the evening that an upset mahout arrived at the cabin with a smug-looking Lilly. She had muffled her bell by stuffing mud into it and had taken off for the plantation as fast as she could.

Nowadays, because their habitat is shrinking, more and more elephants are driven to foraging in farmers' fields and plantations. Much later, I went with Lek to Ban La Ui, a village in the southwest of Thailand close to Burma where many elephants still live in the wild. Some years ago, the traditional harmony that had existed here between man and animal began to fray. So much forest had been cleared for pineapple plantations that the elephants had difficulty in finding enough food so they began to raid the plantations. The villagers had approached Lek to ask if she could find a solution. They had already built huts for guards who would throw fireworks, such as squibs, to keep the elephants at bay. They had also used tame elephants to drive the wild ones away. That evening, we drove into the mountains to size up the situation. Soon we saw elephant dung and stripped trees. '*Chang* around us!' our guide Chom yelled from the roof of the pick-up truck, and suddenly, thirty feet ahead of us, a giant elephant stepped out onto the road. We held our breath, my skin crawled. This was no tame elephant! The next day, Lek told the village leader that they had to solve the problem themselves; they had to stop logging, and find ways to restore peace between mankind and elephant. Plans were made to create a fixed feeding location near the lake where the elephants drink and bathe. The huts for the guards could become observation posts. People would be able to watch wild elephants, and a research team could study the groups of elephants and individual relationships among them. Ecotourism combined with science.

Elephant experts say there is only one real solution to the human-elephant conflict: expanding the protected areas. But government policy tends to bring about the opposite, so I am told. The National Parks, Wildlife, and Plant Conservation Department seems to focus more on tourism than on wild animals, and despite the laws against it, there is a constant nibbling away at the edges of nature parks: the rich build villas, the poor burn down patches of forest for agriculture. Elephants live in 49 of 136 protected areas but in many cases their numbers are too small to survive. In one of those areas, there is only one female left. As long as the elephants' habitat isn't expanded, experts say, local communities have to be involved in protecting wild elephants. This sometimes works. One village decided to adopt a pestering elephant. The villagers drive him off a bit and then let him eat so that their losses are spread out among them. And they now grow more crops that elephants won't eat. Fortunately, our elephants—being well-fed and guarded over by watchful eyes—hardly ever stray onto farming land.

***

Back at The Farm, it's mostly the little elephants that keep me busy. Gingmai is restless at night; he doesn't like to be left alone. I massage him for hours. His eyes keep closing as he fights to stay awake, just like me.

After three weeks, it's hard to say goodbye. I know I will be back. Six months later, I get a message from Thailand. Gingmai is dead, maybe poisoned. Would Lek's enemies really go this far?

2

Complications

A T THE END of 2003, after a year and a half, I finally manage to return. Thailand has never been entirely absent from my thoughts. The determination to do more than just volunteer every now and then and donate money is firmer now. The Elephant Nature Park has also expanded, along with a corresponding need of funds. It now extends over 150-square acres and houses twenty elephants. Then there is Elephant Haven, in the mountain area across the river, which has to be shared with two trekking camps. Lek would very much like to buy the entire area, including the two camps, but she lacks the means to do so. A more realistic goal is the purchase of a smaller plot of land directly across the river; it costs fifty thousand euros. Besides Lek and Pom, there are now twenty mahouts at the Park, a construction team, and housekeeping personnel: a total of about forty employees. In addition to that, there are three foreign staff members and an ever-changing number of volunteers.

On average, supporting an elephant costs three hundred euros a month. Every day, the herd takes over two hundred euros just for food. Money comes in from organisations like the British EleAid, the American Serengeti Foundation, and the Alexander Abraham Foundation, but the bulk of money comes from tourists. Some come as day-trippers, others for a few days, and some for weeks, as volunteers.

The huts for mahouts, volunteers, and guests are pleasant buildings, grouped together around trees. They are on stilts, like all traditional Thai houses. This makes for cool rooms and helps keep all kinds of forest creatures out of doors where they belong. When the river overflows its banks, the huts are not easily flooded. They are almost entirely made of bamboo, which is far cheaper than wood and environmentally friendly. When bamboo is cut down, it grows back quickly as a giant grass, not a tree. Some of the walls are bamboo panels made of long interwoven, flexible laths; others feature interlocking stems sliced length-ways in half, with every other one fitted round side out. The roofs are thatched. There are showers and toilets with running water, with electricity, too. People eat together in the main hut and there's even a television room where Lek plays the video material about the *phajaan* for anyone wanting to watch.

***

This time, I am taking care of Lilly, a slow lady elephant. Her body and mind have been heavily taxed by the logging industry where she spent her entire life dragging logs. She was given drugs so as not to feel the pain. Lek found her on a Jumbo Express expedition. The owner had basically given up on her. It took three months to revive her spirit. Now she wanders around the Park, still slow and as if half-asleep, but the dull look in her eyes that she had one-and-a-half years ago has disappeared, and she is starting to respond to her mahout. When a 'girlfriend' comes around to visit her, she doesn't pointedly ignore her anymore.

Female elephants love family life. In the wild, they live in herds of about twenty elephants. They form close groups and have social lives that a modern city-dweller would envy. The females are in charge. They watch over the little ones, are the role models in daily life, and maintain order and safety within the family group. Bulls, as male elephants are officially called, may sometimes help out a little when it comes to the latter but join the herd mostly during the mating season. They otherwise wander around in loose male gangs or as loners. When a baby is born, the mother chooses one or more 'aunts' to help her in raising it. Young males hang out with the herd until they're about eight years old, then they drift off and find their own way. When an elephant lacks or rejects these social bonds, as Lilly did when she arrived, it is in a bad way.

My days in the Park regain their natural rhythm: making an early start to get fodder ready, clearing out dung, then feeding time, and going to the river for a swim twice a day. Lilly waits patiently for me to clean out her sleeping space. She knows she'll get food afterwards. The first few days, I walk around her carefully while talking to her. When I have heaped the dung, I neatly rake the floor. After a few days, she starts to look at me. I happily keep talking and tell her about my plans. Almost without noticing it myself, I begin to crawl underneath her huge body while raking. I have come to trust her. And she me, a little. She even lays her trunk on my shoulders.

On a scorching hot day, I notice someone sitting underneath Lilly, beside the river. Bochu, her mahout, is cooling down in her shadow. I sit down next to him. 'Lilly is the most special elephant I know,' he says. 'She is so slow and gentle. There are not many elephants who don't mind humans underneath them.'

Bochu speaks English well, as many Burmese do. Most of the mahouts at the Park belong to the Karen tribe that lives scattered throughout much of Burma and northern Thailand. During World War II in Burma, they helped the British, their former colonisers, who promised them autonomy by way of thanks. When they didn't get it, the Karen started a struggle for freedom against the generals who rule Burma with terror. The junta use their own citizens as slave labourers. Any resistance is met with death, or at least imprisonment. Almost half of the national budget is spent on armaments, while the only war waged is the one against their own people.

Bochu comes from a mountain village. He used to be a teacher but became a mahout when he realised he could earn more in logging. 'It was very hard work, from early in the morning until late at night. The elephants had to pull very heavy tree trunks. You had to use the hooked goad—bang, bang—hit the side of the head, hit the forehead.' After a year, Bochu fled to Thailand with five friends. 'We walked at night, we were afraid of the soldiers. If you got caught . . .' He pulls his forefinger, an imaginary knife, across his throat. After two weeks, they crossed the border and ended up in a refugee camp.

There are many Karen refugees in Thailand, some in camps, some working illegally. When they find a job, and want to take some money to their family in the camp, they have to be careful of the military checkpoints along the way. Some arrive penniless, having had to hand everything over. 'At the camp, I met mahouts who had jobs in trekking camps. I got one too, and worked there for three years. Hard work, not much fun.' He likes it much better at Lek's. 'Easygoing, I can work at my own pace and live with other mahouts.' Bochu wants to stay in Thailand and never go back to Burma. 'Life is very expensive there, I can't buy rice.' Then: 'And I have no freedom there.'

His parents died of an illness. He has not spoken to his brothers or sisters in all these years. 'They probably think I'm dead. I would really like to let them know I'm all right. Maybe I'll go to a refugee camp near the border soon. From there I can cross the border in a group.'

'What does your future look like?'

'See my family again. And find love.' Life = love, he draws in the sand. Lilly takes a few steps forward, suddenly the sun beats down on us. We realise we are thirsty and stroll back to the main hut.

***

Maximus arrived at the Park this year. He has to be the biggest elephant I have ever seen. He is about forty-two, and since elephants keep growing all their lives, he's still got a way to go. Max, as he is soon called, has suffered a lot. His mother worked in logging in the northwestern province of Tak. Max was taken from her and sold at an early age. He grew up to become one of the largest elephants in Thailand. This was first recognised when his mahout took him to Bangkok. Because of his size, he was a big hit with the tourists. Pictures of him can probably be found all over the world. When the government started a campaign in 1999 to keep the elephants out of the city, Max was affected with all the other street elephants. Working illegally meant they were out on the streets at night, then hiding out of sight during the day, somewhere at the edge of the city. Max and his mahout lived next to a rubbish dump.

When life in Bangkok became impossible, they moved to Chonburi, a seaside resort south of Bangkok. There, they left their campsite on a hot April night and headed into town. In the darkness, a lorry crashed into Max from behind and rammed him along for quite a distance. The mahout, spared because he was walking beside his elephant, took Max home to the northeast where he fought to save his life for a long time. He took care of him as well as he could but he lacked the money for medical treatment, and Max never fully recovered; his right front leg remained stiff.

A year later, the limping giant had to return to work in Bangkok. Then, at a festival, he caught the eye of a British couple familiar with Lek's work. They bought Max in the spring of 2003 and took him to the Elephant Nature Park. He is still suffering and needs a lot of medication.

***

The Park is a book filled with sad stories. No matter how good it feels to see all those happy endings here, I just couldn't stop worrying. No elephant should be subjected to what happened to Max, what was done to Lilly, what Jabu has had to deal with in her young life. I wanted to do something to eradicate the evil, to get elephants off the street once and for all. Then, during one of my last nights, sitting around the campfire at Elephant Haven with Pom, the project called *Bring the elephant home* was born: a plan to liberate two street elephants and make a statement by walking from Bangkok to the Park, creating support for ecotourism with elephants and drawing attention to the Elephant Nature Park. I lay the plan out for the staff, very carefully, because I'm afraid they'll call it naive and unrealistic. In the meantime, I have backed it up with a provisional cost estimate, the route, and a sponsoring and publicity plan. The response is enthusiastic. If I really want to do this, it can be done and they will support me.

***

The preparations back home in the Netherlands for *Bring the elephant home* last eighteen months and I have never been so stressed. I get off to a good start. I browse the Internet for street elephants and save all the information to make sure I have done my homework. Street elephants appear to be a fairly recent phenomenon. Sometimes they carry tourists, but more often they beg for money or food, obliged to do this by their mahouts. The animals sleep on wasteland near the fringes of the city, often next to rubbish dumps, and trudge along congested roads and through traffic jams. They are generally undernourished, while their feet get seared, tenderised, and bruised on the fiercely heated tarmac. The city noise assaults their sensitive ears, and the vibrations from the traffic are frightening because they feel these through their feet. Elephants are generally gregarious animals, so such urban isolation is traumatic.

The Thai government, and the senior administrators of large cities like Bangkok, have tried to end it. The governor of Bangkok even once suggested shooting all street elephants. There have even been failed attempts to retrain the animals along with their mahouts to work as foresters in protected nature reserves. Since 2003, there has been a law prohibiting begging with elephants, if only because they contribute to traffic jams. But it has not proved possible to enforce it.

The degradation of the once so highly respected elephant is primarily due to the swirling pace of the modernisation of Thailand since 1950. While the country has become an important exporter of agricultural produce, it has industrialised as well. Nature and the environment have suffered in the process. In the 1950s, sixty-five percent of northeastern Thailand was covered with forest; in 1981 only eight percent of this remained. Sadly enough, the elephants themselves played a prominent role in this deforestation. They were used to extract the high-value timber, hauling the massive logs out of the jungle. The national forestry organisation praised them as 'the majestic animals of the Thai teak logging industry'. As recently as 1974, twelve thousand elephants worked in the forest.

In 1989, after a whole village was buried by a mudslide resulting from deforestation, a complete ban on logging was promulgated. For the wild elephants this was a blessing, since what was left of their habitat would now remain intact, in theory. In actual fact, the remaining forests are constantly under pressure. But the new legislation caused a sudden massive lay-off of mahouts and their elephants by the logging industry. As it turned out, they soon found alternative careers in illegal logging and in the tourist industry.

In early 1900, before modernisation, Thailand had an estimated hundred thousand elephants. Now only an estimated fifteen hundred remain in the wild and two thousand work with humans. Most nature treks are bad for the animals because they are being worked to death and are given inadequate medical care. But the animals in the cities and on the beaches are worse off. The mahouts, usually from a tribe that has kept elephants for centuries and considers them family, often do have their hearts in the right place. But because their home region has been stripped virtually bare of forests and can support neither humans nor elephants any longer, they have become migrant workers in the cities. Big businessmen see elephants begging as a profitable affair. They own dozens of elephants and hire them out to mahouts. These elephants miss out even on the last bit of safety a caring mahout can give them.

I find it strange in a Buddhist society, where respect for life is strongly felt, that the elephant has been turned into nothing more than a means of making money. Of old, it was a sacred animal, inseparable from Thailand's history. Elephants helped win wars. Now these former heroes lumber along the streets, fenced in between fenders in traffic jams, a plastic bag tied to each one's tail as a cheap reflector.

***

19

During our trek, I want to direct a spotlight to this abuse. I want to talk to the local population, to monks, teachers, children, politicians, and journalists. I want to discover what is left of the traditional respect for elephants. I want to create support for the preservation of their habitat and to encourage new forms of ecotourism.

It will all be in the business plan I'm working on; the second one in my life I'll be putting my heart into. When I eventually submit it to Lek, my professional attitude convinces her and she gives it the green light. She even tries to find allies among Thai politicians. Roger, a collaborator of the ENP office in Chiang Mai, becomes my coordinator in Thailand. We discuss the broad outline of the route, the minimal number of people on the team, and the materials we need. And above all the budget. Roger adds some more things to the list of expenses and corrects the amounts. Oops! The total is now fifty thousand euros. Ten thousand of this is for maintaining the freed elephants after their arrival at the Park. We might be able to deduct ten thousand from the remainder if I can get material sponsorship in kind. That leaves thirty thousand euros to be gathered before the launch. That seems do-able. After all, I am a fundraiser.

***

Bring the elephant home goes public at a festival of Friends of the Elephant, which is an organisation dedicated to improving the lives of elephants, both in Africa and Asia. It also supports the Elephant Nature Park. When I take the plan to Rob Faber, its dynamic chairman, he is all for it. 'Well, what are we waiting for?' he says. In three weeks, his gang is organising an elephant festival. A splendid opportunity to tell the world about *Bring the elephant home* and to find supporters. That means, uh . . . I'd better get going!

I design a leaflet and have it photocopied at a print shop. I send appeals for sponsorship to notaries, website builders, online newsletter makers, printers, and designers. Night after night, I work on a website that still looks feeble. A friend and I paint the logo, an elephant walking away from the city, on a banner. There will have to be statutes and a business bank account. And, of course, any self-respecting foundation visits a notary and the Chamber of Commerce. Three weeks is simply not enough time to take care of everything, but by the time the festival comes round we are in our booth, proud and a little dazed.

My parents, who have not taken me very seriously up to now, come by. 'Whose booth is this exactly?' my mother asks. That night we count the money in the collection-box: ninety-three euros. Thirty contributors have signed on, half of them with a monthly pledge. Not a bad start for a foundation that officially doesn't yet exist.

Then things get sticky. I produce a media plan, plus one for sponsorship and one for fundraising. I mail thirty-five extensive funding requests. I get thirty-four rejections. 'We only support animals in the wild', '. . . only projects in the Netherlands', 'if you had an agency in Thailand . . . ', 'the project is structurally unsound', 'the organisation is too young', 'there's too little initiative from the local population'. The project is too small, too big, too political, not political enough. One environment-friendly bank, though, donates a thousand euros, preventing me from losing heart completely. My estimate that funding would provide half the money needed was obviously a little over-optimistic. Now the individual ten-euro-contributors are going to have to come up with thirty thousand euros. Hmpf.

But there are some rays of hope. Every year, the colleagues of the Friends of the Earth donate their Christmas bonus to a good cause, and this year they choose the elephants: eight hundred euros. Two separate contributors donate a thousand euros each. Sponsors for materials pop up too, with small companies being especially generous. I get a free professional website and e-newsletter, a laptop with accessories, a satellite phone, a flyer designed and printed for free, and hiking shoes. A number of media outlets express interest. I give interviews to several Dutch newspapers and magazines, and to a radio broadcaster. Nature Conservation Films, a production agency for nature films, wants to do a documentary about the trip. Very slowly, the number of contributors increases.

Then Lek sends me an e-mail. '*Yesterday I got a call from someone at EleAid Great Britain, who led the* Bring the elephant home *project two years ago . . . He told me a friend informed him about your website, and that you copied most of the subject and the goal from his website. He asked me to contact you and let you know that he and his girlfriend are very angry . . .*'

A *Bring the elephant home* project two years ago? My stomach turns. I contact the outraged Brits. 'Do you know what you're doing? Three years ago my girlfriend and I bought two street elephants and started a trek to the Elephant Nature Park. We had to stop because our permits were inadequate, and we were being threatened by animal rights people who didn't want us to walk along the roads with the elephants. We feared for our lives. If you want to continue anyway, go to India, where the issue of the elephants isn't as controversial and political.'

It feels like a bomb has dropped right beside me and I'm left trembling at the edge of the crater. How is this possible? Why didn't I know this? But when I call Lek, she is surprised. Didn't I know? That's where the project's name came from, didn't it? Well, no, that had popped up after a lot of beer at the camp fire . . . Lek doesn't take it too seriously. 'We'll just explain to them that we will do things differently this time.' When I express my worries about the fiasco of the first trip, she tries to reassure me. 'At that time the *phajaan* video had just been released. Everything we set out to do was being sabotaged. This time things will be different, better thought out, better prepared, with better circumstances. We know what to expect now, it can't go wrong.'

I summon up my courage. At least Thailand is still with it. Although it is too bad that for now Thailand means only the people of the Elephant Nature Park. There has been no answer to my letters to the Thai governmental departments, the Tourism Authority of Thailand, the media, and the animal organisations, while our most urgent priorities now lie with securing permits and a favourable public opinion. 'Let everybody see clearly that you want to work with and for the local population,' project coordinator Roger writes. 'Show empathy, not an accusing finger.'

The affair makes a dent in my confidence that is hard to repair. When I feel really down I often go to the Amsterdam Zoo to sit with the elephants for a while. I always climb over the outer fence, as I don't want to support this zoo by paying the entrance fee. The elephant accommodation is too bare; there is one male, almost always on his own, and two females that, of course, cannot form a group. The visits fire me up, I always leave more determined to carry on.

In May, a campaign offer drops from the sky that seems tailor-made to solve all the money problems. A mobile communications company offers four people the opportunity to realise their dreams. They will get an annual salary, twenty-five thousand euros for expenses and communication equipment. It is about projects that 'can make a difference'; small, unique initiatives that require courage and passion. This is *Bring the elephant home*, we're made for the part! Four hundred plans are submitted, we are in the final twenty. This can't go wrong. And then a short e-mail: sorry, no go.

I am having a hard time. I should never have started this, I don't want to do this anymore. Why can't someone just donate ten thousand euros? Doubt and insecurity shoot up like poisonous fungi. Everybody tries to cheer me up, but after all the oodles of energy expended there is still only seven thousand euros in the bank.

But then halfway through 2005, the tide begins turning. The association against laboratory experiments on animals mails our flyer out along with their newsletter, for free. Forty thousand animal lovers reached at one go! After that, contributors keep calling in. During the first few days, there are on average at least fifty envelopes in my letterbox. Every time I cycle home from work, I'm already imagining the euphoric letterbox moment. The plans for the Nature Conservation Films documentary are taking a more definite shape as well.

***

At the end of every day her mahout starts out with Boonrod from beside the rubbish dump where she lives during the day, and takes her into the busy Chiang Mai night scene. There she begs until all the bars and discos close. Drunks pull on her tail and try to make her drink beer. When Boonrod hungrily reaches out with her trunk to a restaurant table for leftovers, a customer throws hot coffee in her face. The mahout does nothing. He isn't the owner, he rents the little elephant to make a living.

On the evening of July 18, Boonrod walks around with bags of bananas on her back. Suddenly the police arrive, determined to uphold the law this time. The mahout climbs on Boonrod and uses his elephant hook: go, go! She panics and runs about aimlessly; the mahout jumps to the ground and takes off without her. She bumps into a motorbike, then into a car, and after that walks right through an outdoor café. It takes the police five hours to catch her. Finally, they call the Elephant Nature Park. Afterwards she is taken to the Park in a truck. For the first time in her life, her days are all about food and play, for the first time she is part of a herd. Three days later, the owner and the mahout are at the Park. The police business has been taken care of, Boonrod has to go back to work.

When Lek runs into her again on the street two weeks later, her leg swollen because of a recent car accident, she decides on the spot to take her to the Park. She calls for a truck, tells the mahout he can come and work at the Park if he wants, and loads Boonrod into the truck. Thanks to a gift from a British conservation organisation, the owner can be financially compensated. But he doesn't want to sell the elephant. After a long to-and-fro palaver, the compromise that emerges is that Boonrod can stay at the Park and that Lek will give the owner some money from time to time.

Through a supporter, some unsettling news arrives. A Thai animal protection organisation has come out against the *Bring the elephant home*. When we start out they will attack. They have informed the police and have asserted that the trip should be stopped, and stated they will alert the press as well. The events of two years ago seem to be repeating themselves. Rumour has it that 'some westerners are about to take elephants for a long haul along the highways in the hot sun for months'. Furthermore, the money we have set aside for the purchase would be far too much. Only a young elephant that knows lots of tricks would be worth the eight thousand euros we are willing to pay, according to the website. In passing, they lash out at Lek. She is alleged to have upped the price to line her own pockets. After all, she is the daughter of a trekking camp owner, a notorious elephant trader, isn't she?

I am busy preparing a benefit festival and couldn't even find time to mend a bicycle puncture, let alone deal with this. I think I can refute the arguments, but I feel afraid and wretched. What have I got myself into? How can I deal with these power games? What do they mean, 'attack'? Why didn't they contact me before they called the police? Maybe I can't do the walk after all, but then what?

So many questions, but no time to look for answers. Friend and colleague Rob cheers me up. 'Attack? Don't be silly! You're going to take your elephants for a walk, no one can object to that. It's just jealousy, you don't have to change your plans because of that. You intend well, trust that.'

I write to Lek. 'We'll go and talk to this organisation together,' she writes back, 'with a lawyer present.' We can't do anything yet, though, you'll have to come back to Thailand first.' Since I can't do anything yet, I cheer up and get on with the festival preparations. The affair keeps haunting me, though. Don't think about it, time is running out, we still have to conjure up ten thousand euros, I tell myself.

***

For a whole week, the activities at the Theresia School in Rotterdam are all about elephants. Banners in the windows, clay elephants, paper elephants, drawings, paintings, and stories. I come by and am bombarded with questions. Can we give you bandages for the elephants in Thailand? If you buy a male and a female, maybe they will have a baby and the elephants won't go extinct! Are elephants afraid of mice? Do they ever throw up? Don't they scare you? Will you be on television? Can they lift a human with their tusks? Do they cry? How do they talk? The children begin to ponder their own abilities to change the world a bit. And at the end of the week, the school donates 2,114 euros.

To boost the steadily growing bank account some more, we come up with the benefit festival *Elephantasia*. What started out as a party becomes a happening with two stages, seven bands, three deejays, ten acts, a market, and an auction. All of August is taken up with the preparations. Friends, colleagues, contributors, sponsors, everyone is recruited. Blijburg, a small easygoing beach spa on the IJ lake near Amsterdam, is available. We can do whatever we like, the two women in charge say.

Without many expectations I send an e-mail to the singer Heather Nova, one of my all-time heroes. Would she like to come and sing at Blijburg, since she will be in Holland anyway for the Lowlands Music Festival? I am stunned to get an e-mail from Bermuda that same night. 'Great project, I would love to help.' I am so excited I can't sleep. In the end it's not possible to synchronise our calendars, but my meeting with her at the Lowlands festival is one of my personal highlights. Heather becomes ambassador-at-large of *Bring the elephant home*, and she also donates an autographed copy of her collection of poems and signed copies of her new album for the auction. Famous cartoonists put their original drawings at our disposal, as well as signed copies of their new books. An author draws a picture for us in his latest book. In a short while, *Elephantasia* is everywhere in Amsterdam; on posters, in trams, in magazines and newspapers. With three days to go, Blijburg calls. They have messed up the permits, the festival is off, they don't see a way out. The next day I try to get the chairman of the city district on the phone, in vain. But they don't know me yet! When it comes to elephants, I can move mountains. I jump on my bicycle, and am soon sitting down with the chairman and the officials responsible. I am presented with an example of the Dutch culture of tolerant flexibility. A permit is absolutely impossible, but they are willing to help in making the festival run smoothly.

On September 3, the weather is beautiful. The beach is packed. The bands play until crests dance on the waves, even without a permit. In a wooden stand, visitors are enjoying a Thai massage, while further along the beach the Kamasutra Machine by Porno&Pardon is running at full speed. A circus without animals, eroticism without nudes, exoticism without bananas, and safety without condoms—it's all possible! For five euros, you can get a sailing lesson along with rosé wine; the romantic boats sail back and forth across the lake. After the Thai buffet—the best cuisine in the world—the day on the beach ends with a huge camp fire. Just before closing time, Miss Wanna-be-a-Star and Miss Behave do a pole dancing act. When everything is finally over, I sleepwalk to my tent on the beach and pass out in a very pleasant way. Meanwhile, when the accounts are totted up, we have added another four thousand euros. The next morning we clean up the beach in the hot sun. 'I feel like I've just spent a week in a prison camp,' a volunteer says when we turn into the street where we are going to unload the truck after the final trip.

***

During the week before departure, I only need to take care of some practical things—clearing out my room, going to the doctor's for health formalities, securing a credit card, getting the laptop with satellite connection ready. Everything is under control. Until, that is, I receive an e-mail from Lek. Typhoon Damrey—Cambodian for 'elephant'—has crossed northern Thailand. The storm and the floods have destroyed half of the Elephant Nature Park. The team has taken the elephants and the other animals to a higher part of the Park, but the buildings and farm lands have been severely damaged. Some of the mahouts have lost everything they owned.

My mind is spinning. What are the consequences? Will there be a Park left to walk to? Shouldn't we use the money we collected to rebuild the Park? My project now has no top priority. Don't think about it too much for now. Let's get there first. But after banning the Park from my mind, I start worrying about myself. I don't want to leave everybody behind and go to Thailand alone. Or yes, I want to go, but not with an airplane full of expectations. And maybe there are no elephants in the streets anymore. The missing permits and the Thai attacks on my project zigzag through my sleepless nights. My housemate Sofie shows me a cartoon of a girl with a monstrous suitcase getting off the underground railway in a big city. The text balloon above her head says: 'Is this what I really want?' We get the giggles and drink too much wine. I'll just go and bring these elephants home, I think, no one can stop me now. We'll just bribe everybody. 'Hire armed mahouts and fight your way through Thailand,' is Sofie's final advice. Before I fall asleep, I think of the worst thing that could happen. Something with the elephants, that would be the worst thing. Or to be arrested and tortured in a Thai prison, that's bad too. Some media attention that would produce! Perhaps that would bring in enough money to ransom all the street elephants. I dream of a gloomy street party. There's fire, an elephant, people are yelling. The elephant panics and storms into the crowd. I try to run after it to calm it down, but I fail.

3

Whether You Like It or Not

WITH MY BACKPACK and laptop I walk to the taxi stand outside Don Muang, the 'Old' Bangkok International Airport. I have an appointment with the Dutch ambassador in the afternoon. I believe it is important to tell him about the project. Who knows, maybe he can help? If I end up in prison, for example. The ambassador welcomes me kindly and enthusiastically. But he confirms my fears. 'Thai don't like meddlesome foreigners. You'll have to take that into account.' He gives me practical tips, and says I can call him at all times.

In the evening, I go to a get-together of the Dutch Society in The Blue Elephant, a classy club. It is slightly beyond my means, but it's easy to start a conversation. 'So you work with animals? How nice, so do I! I am a product manager in the chicken industry. Right now we're developing a product that'll beat the Thai chicken.' He knows where to find street elephants in Bangkok. I write down the addresses. Next table. Wife of a businessman, voluntary teacher at an international school. 'Elephant lessons? At our school? Priceless! I don't think so.' Laughing, I leave The Blue Elephant.

There is an elephant theme park in Samphran, an hour's drive from Bangkok. The tame giants play soccer and dance, they play war and drag logs around. You can take a tour on their backs through a plastic jungle. There are many baby elephants. They dance, play the drums, stand on their hind legs, and even on their heads. Elephants can learn up to thirty tricks; they never forget and live to an old age, so follow the money.

After the show, they walk among the audience. I am filming when one of them approaches me. The little elephants at the Elephant Nature Park would definitely seize the opportunity to push me over or take the camera from me. This little elephant just checks me for something to eat. Would it ever have been playful? I manage to go 'backstage', and see the stars of the show in their separate concrete pens.

Fig 1. En route for Elephant Haven

Fig 2. Antoinette swims with Gingmai, Hope, and Jabu (photo: Karl Cullen)

Fig 3. Boonkhum near the hut in Elephant Haven

Fig 4. Street elephant Fong Peng in Bangkok

Fig 5. Street elephant Oem Bon in Bangkok

Fig 6. Lek and the herd in the Elephant Nature Park

Fig 7. Stocking up on elephant snacks with Pom

Fig 8. Enter the elephants, Surin festival

Fig 9. Elephant with howdah and goad, Surin festival

Fig 10. Surin festival

Fig 11. Audience, Surin festival

Fig 12. Elephants collect money, Surin festival

Fig 13. Mahouts and elephants camp on the outskirts of Bangkok

At night, I go to the Bangkok city centre, looking for street elephants. I'm armed with photo and film cameras, and the list of street names from the chicken manager: Nana, Patpong, Soi Cowboy, Asoke, Sukhumvit Soi 2 and 7. A *tuktuk* seems to be the best means of transportation. The three-wheeled scooter taxi sputters and smells, but it'll take you everywhere. 'You want to feed bananas to elephant?' the driver asks. Along the way he tells me there aren't many street elephants at the moment, because of recent police raids. 'But they'll all be back within a month. Especially when the dry season starts and the mahouts have no more work in their villages.'

We criss-cross at speed through the traffic; every now and then the driver stops to ask passers-by whether they have seen any elephants. He tries very hard. It's wonderful to be back in Bangkok and race around in the sultry night. I used to have a lot of fun here as a tourist. Now I'm on a mission and it's even more fun. After twenty minutes I spot an elephant of about eight years old. 'Stop! There!' A screech of breaks, and I jump out of the still moving vehicle, cameras at the ready. The mahout sits on the elephant and yells that I have to give some money. The girl next to them tries to sell me bananas. The driver is trying to calm the situation. The three of them are talking to me, but I hardly hear them, all I can see is the elephant and I try to keep him in the middle of the viewfinder. Then the trio walks off, right through the heavy traffic of Asoke. At least one of my worries seems to be unnecessary, there are street elephants, so my project is still useful.

***

On the train to Chiang Mai, the flooded Park looms over me like a dark cloud. Everyone will be down and out of course, with everything in pieces and half the land swept away. And here I come with my plans for two extra elephants. At the same time, I feel the weight of the expectations, of all those people who believe in me. I don't want to do this anymore! But I must. After all those dreams, all the work, I just can't let it fail.

Usually, when I panic because I am stuck over things, I start thinking about something else. Something I would like to do. So I begin thinking about the second benefit festival that I'll be organising in Holland. I start making a scenario and checklists. Structure creates a sense of control. I fantasise about a test walk from Chiang Mai to the Park. We'll just do everything on a small scale first, with simple permits and logistics. This way we'll build up experience and confidence. What a plan! I share a bottle of beer—Chang beer, of course, with elephants on the label—with my Thai neighbour opposite. He teaches at Chiang Mai University and invites me to go on a weekend trip with his students to the Golden Triangle, the tract of land taking in parts of Thailand, Burma and Laos, famous for its opium smuggling. Unfortunately, my next few days are fully booked. When we reach Chiang Mai, the professor takes me to my guesthouse, gives me his cellphone number and his wife's, and tells me I can call him day or night. Thailand is the best country in the whole wide world.

At the Elephant Nature Park office, there is nothing but joy. Lek is going to be given the much talked-about and eminent 'Hero of Asia' award, established by Time Magazine and meant to highlight the efforts of ordinary people who do extraordinary things and thus become an inspiration for others. Lek's days as an outcast are over. Journalists call her day and night and even a princess, the king's sister, has contacted her. The personal secretary was forced to call twice, Lek giggles, because the staff member who had taken the call from 'the Palace' on the phone, believing it to be a restaurant, had hung up on them.

We talk about the latest developments of my project. Lek has started to think big. To win the permits that remain outstanding, we will visit Prime Minister Thaksin, she says. 'I will write a project proposal in Thai and request an appointment. If we can get Thaksin to support us, all doors will open. Then we won't have to apply for provincial permits anymore.' We can fall back on a lawyer when it comes to judicial matters, and Pom has arranged for a manager, Mr. Lee, a man with experience and political insight. Pom will also find mahouts.

My anxiety melts away. I don't even propose the test walk anymore, we'll just go for it now.

The little ones at the Park have grown immensely; there are several new elephants, among them as many as five babies. The youngest, Kanoon, is the first baby born at the Park, a month and a half ago. Boonrod, the street elephant from Chiang Mai, immediately took up with him and follows him everywhere, like a protective big sister. Together, they run through the grass. Boonrod is sparkling with energy, she seems to have left the memories of the numbing nightlife of Chiang Mai way behind.

Kanoon's mother Jobaan had given birth twice before. The first baby died at birth due to bad conditions. The second was born healthy, but ended up in the water when playing next to Jobaan, who stood chained near the river. He was swept away by the river and drowned. When things seemed to be going wrong again before Kanoon's birth, the owner took Jobaan to the Park. But bad things are in store for Jobaan and Kanoon. The Park didn't buy them, the owner is only using it as a temporary stable. He wants Jobaan to give birth again as soon as possible, as babies bring in money.

The flood has swept away a piece of land and a new compound. Pastures have turned into rough plains. Flash floods have happened more often over the past fifty years. Because of the deforestation of the mountain slopes, not enough trees are left to retain water and soil with their roots. When it rains and a storm is blowing, the water gushes down the slopes fast and with great force.

But the mud flat left behind by the river on the Park's remaining land is fertile; one can see the grass re-appearing. And the people are just as resilient. With the materials that were salvaged, new huts have been built. Along the river, poles have been hammered into the ground, with sandbags behind them. Thanks to the fast repairs, tourists and volunteers are already returning. In a few months, the river bed will be deepened and rocks will be put along the banks, with help from machines provided by the Thai government. The Park will most likely be able to stay on this site. But more land will have to be bought, not just for giving the elephants space, but for growing food.

I hang out with the elephants all day. In the evening, Pom and I go to a ceremony in a village where several of the mahouts were born. It is a rite of 'making merit'. Through offerings to monks and other good deeds, so Buddhists believe, the chances for a better next life improve. In the village, a plastic tree has been decorated with gifts for the monks. I see plates, cutlery, a flashlight, a packet of batteries, a role of toilet paper with a ribbon around it, lighters, candy, and money. It looks a bit like a Christmas tree. The floor is covered with dishes of curry and other foods, from which the cats steal the chicken meat. Nobody minds. 'Good for the cats, good for karma,' Pom says. She loves cats. Mahouts offer me food and drink and talk to me in Thai. They keep asking Pom if I am staying around longer this time.

***

Lek walks through the Park with a host of cameras trailing her. For Channel 7 and ITV, national television channels, she demonstrates how baby elephants are trained with love instead of with cruelty. For the first time, the Thai press don't treat her as a rebel but as a hero. The ITV-team films all week for a long documentary. All the accusations Lek has had to endure have been checked, and even the images of the *phajaan*, the 'crushing' of the elephant's will, will be broadcast. Now that she's got the chance to tell her story to the whole of Thailand, she's feistier than ever. We are worried. 'Slow down, do you want everyone up in arms again?' But Lek doesn't want to hear us. 'I've had to keep quiet for three years. Now it's my turn. My enemies have killed Gingmai, now is the time I can stand up for him.'

During an interview with Channel 7, she calls me in. 'You have to say something about the difference between a commercial elephant show and the elephants here.' I talk about the baby elephants in Samphran, about how they had lost their playfulness and wander around by themselves, without a protective mother or aunt nearby. Elephants in their natural surroundings are really much more fun than in a show like that, I trumpet enthusiastically. And of course I seize the opportunity to get *Bring the elephant home* into the living rooms. After one week in Thailand, we're already on national TV!

Apparently my foreign meddling is all right now, because ITV also wants to interview me. Toom will question me. He is a movie star and breathtakingly beautiful. Some Thai men are so feminine, so graceful and slender. When he introduces himself, all blow-dried and made-up, I feel a little uncomfortable in my elephant-tending gear. We sit beside the river watching the splashing elephants, talk about the Park and about my project. Toom thinks it interesting that someone from a country without them would want to help elephants.

The taping takes place in one of the bamboo huts. It's not exactly a cross-examination. I'm prepared for the one critical question from Toom. 'Are you against making money with elephants?' 'Just the opposite', I say. 'Mahouts need money to provide for their elephants. During the project we want to raise interest in animal-friendly ecotourism, like the Elephant Nature Park.' 'On behalf of all of Thailand, thank you,' Toom says. It's going all right, not bad at all.

Reactions to the broadcast are positive. Despite the images of the *phajaan*, despite Lek attacking the people who killed Gingmai. Apparently, it has become impossible to ignore her. The phone is ringing off the hook, the Park is receiving lots of donations, and even more press is coming in.

Elephant Haven is always green, but now the rains have turned it into a lush Garden of Eden. The elephants disappear immediately. In the evening I help

Pom cook. Peeling bamboo, shredding mushrooms, picking basil leaves. The mahouts laugh at me when I try to make curry paste with a mortar. 'A Thai mother judges her future daughter-in-law by the way she uses a mortar. You wouldn't stand a chance,' Pom says. When dinner is done, she tells an elephant story from the Karen tribe.

'A man slaughters a cow and has so much meat he has to store it. He salts it, then he fills hollow bamboo stems with it and plugs them up carefully. His wife is not allowed to touch it. Being jealous and curious, one day she opens one of the bamboo stems, in which a fly has been caught by accident. It flies into her nose and the woman starts to sneeze. The fly is stuck. The woman is sneezing and sneezing until her nose starts to grow. It gets longer and heavier, causing her body to lean forward. Her arms get bigger to be able to support her body. And she becomes incredibly hungry. She eats so much she keeps getting bigger and can't live in the house anymore. She complains to her husband: "Why do you leave me outside? Why don't I get more food?" Because she keeps trying to get into the house, her husband chains her foot to a tree. Now she is eating so much, the husband can't keep up anymore. He has her work in the logging industry.'

I think it is a silly story. Unfriendly to women and elephants. Just like the Thai proverb I heard the other day: 'A man is like the front legs of an elephant, a woman is like its hind legs. What do you mean hind legs? The female always leads the herd!'

At the campfire we sing the Thai elephant song. '*Chang chang chang, nong kheoi hen chang ru plao. Chang man tuo to mai bao. Chamuk yao yao, riak wa nguang. Mi khieo tai nguang, riak wa nga. Mi hu mi ta, hang yao.*' That's difficult. I write down the translation, perhaps that way I'll remember. 'Elephant, elephant, elephant, have you ever seen an elephant before? Elephant is big, not small. Long, long nose, called trunk. Big teeth under trunk, called tusks. Has ears, has eyes, long tail.' It's the first song Thai children learn in school; it will have an important place in the school programme we will do on our walk.

Two years ago Pom and I came up with our wild plan here. 'You aren't just a volunteer, you're one of us,' Pom said then. 'Stay here and help us, your heart is with the Park, isn't it?' 'I can't stay, I have my life in Amsterdam. But I'll be back as soon as possible.' 'And then you'll visit us again for a few weeks? Is that what you want?' I wanted more. Now I'm almost there. I crawl into my sleeping bag near the campfire. I look at the stars, I hear the sounds of the forest, I feel the heat of the fire.

The next day Lilly is missing. Bochu spends a day and a night looking for her before he finds her. She has been walking and eating the whole time. She looks good, much better than Bochu. It's almost as if she's laughing up her sleeve.

***

The food supply for the twenty-six elephants at the Park is problematic. Mahouts collect grass in the area, but that is not without risk. At an elephant camp nearby, thirteen elephants have died recently after eating grass that most likely contained too many pesticides. The vegetables and fruits from the market aren't safe either; we wash them down with salt, but that's just a makeshift measure. Moreover, market fruit is expensive. More farming land of our own is the only solution. On behalf of *Bring the elephant home*, I give Lek two thousand euros, with which she buys a banana plantation. A forest of large trees on a beautiful hill. That's what I call a sustainable investment.

With at least as much satisfaction, I invest my own money in two entirely different animals. Lek drives into the Park with a little light brown bullock with moist eyes in the back of the pick-up truck. On the way to the slaughterhouse, he jumped from a moving truck, in which he stood along side his sister. We nurse his wounds and try to keep Jungle Boy, one of the younger elephants, away from him. His curious trunk almost pulls an ear from the bullock's head. We put the animal behind a fence to recover. Lek calls the owner and tells him he can bring his other calf to the Park as well. A young animal on it's own will just be lonely among the elephants. Once it arrives at the Park, the calf moos and runs to her brother. Then they both calm down and sniff each other down. I decide to adopt them and call them Vegi and Teri. Saved from the slaughterhouse, forever. The mahouts build a bamboo cow barn in short order.

I put a message on the website and get responses from Holland immediately. 'Stay focused, will you? You're over there to buy elephants, not cows.' 'Just save your money and your energy for the elephants. Cows are not endangered.' 'Walking with two calves is a lot cheaper.' I don't blame them. Everybody is waiting for the purchase of elephants, and I give them calves.

In Chiang Mai, I rent an apartment, simple and cheap, but it does have wireless Internet. I don't just use my laptop to work out plans, but also as a phone, mailbox, press agency, administrative office, photo album, music player, cinema, diary, and for website maintenance. I had no idea how valuable such a thing could be in foreign parts.

E-mail is a daily anchor. There are headache messages and cheer-me-ups, like the one from Marjolein of Nature Conservation Films. Animal Planet is interested in a documentary on *Bring the elephant home*. Marjolein wants to come to Thailand in November, together with a crew, and film the purchase of the elephants.

Chiang Mai's nightlife may not be suitable for elephants, but I like it just fine. There's a small restaurant along the river where local bands perform. They mainly play covers of Western underground rock, my kind of music. Everyone is sitting in groups around tables, a bottle of Mekong whiskey in the middle. You're always invited. *Regina* is one of my favourite places. It's a restaurant behind a store where Thai art treasures and knick-knacks collect dust together. Passing through that, you end up in a garden where you can eat. The river murmurs, it's always quiet. I prefer to sit in the large armchair in the middle of the garden, where you can sit to read and write. A rooster and a chicken keep me company, I name them Gerrit and Mathilde. Mathilde bullies Gerrit all day long. When I scatter some food, Mathilde is the first one there. The early bird, suddenly I get the meaning of that expression. But in the evening, when Gerrit crows at the top of his voice, Mathilde always watches him with pride and contentment.

Without much enthusiasm, I work my way through permit country. I hate it, I hate it! According to our plans, we'll be buying elephants in two weeks and we're not even allowed to walk with hamsters, let alone elephants. We don't have permission to do anything. The Thai project proposal is now with the secretary's office of the Prime Minister, we try to get an appointment. I am largely relying on Lek. She is in frequent contact with the princess, who asked her 'what that Dutch woman is doing', and told her to bring me by some day. After an explanation, the princess magnanimously promised her support. 'But when will we have an audience with her, Lek? Shouldn't we be able to manage those permits with her help?' Patience and confidence, that's what I should exercise. The world of Thai officialdom can sometimes be unbearably 'sticky'.

Lek tells me to buy proper clothes. My jeans are absolutely unsuitable for visiting lawyers and Rotary Clubs, let alone the princess. Everybody in the office butts in. A skirt, not too short, but tight, with a Thai feel to it . . . and I have always despised shopping for clothes. Lek sends along her friend Oi. I don't like anything we see, except for one expensive black wrinkly silk dress. Three shop employees dress me, add a thin scarf to cover my shoulders, jewellery, glittery shoes, hair let down, and suddenly I'm chic. Oi has me walk through the store. 'You walk like an elephant! Walk like a lady now. You can't walk like this if you're meeting the princess!' Eight people have gathered around me by now. What is this about a princess? Who is this celebrity? At the office everybody sits up in surprise as well. 'Wow,' Lek says, 'if we go to Thaksin like this, he'll write those permits personally.'

That evening we're expected at the Rotary Club. I am late because my laptop automatically changed to Dutch wintertime, which doesn't apply in Thailand. Pom calls me to ask what's up, I jump on my rented scooter and race to the office as fast as I dare. The rain is pouring down. Within a few minutes, I'm soaking wet. The silk dress sticks to my body, my hair hangs in wet strings down my face. At the office Pom, doubled over with laughter, opens the door of the spin-dryer: 'You go inside!' No Rotary for me tonight.

***

Lee, the manager-to-be, is an old school friend of Lek's. He used to have very long hair, down to his waist. He cut it short when he started working as a security guard in the Royal Palace in Saudi Arabia. He's had a restaurant in Japan as well. Nowadays he is a farmer, an organic farmer. Together with his father and brothers he has a tamarind orchard, among other things. Lee loves animals, not just elephants but all animals. He works and lives with his heart, he says. On our trek he will take care of communications with local authorities, contact school leaders and temple monks, take care of food and materials, manage the mahouts, and translate the elephant lessons at the schools. Lee inspires confidence. He suggests a drive along the route we'll be walking, to be able to make detailed plans, scout out campsites, and get to know the local population.

The person who does not inspire confidence at all is the lawyer. He acts interested, asks for details and says he wants to help. He claims he can take on all the paperwork. He works for a street dog advocacy organisation. His price: 430 euros per elephant. By Thai standards that's greedy. Lek calls him a 'bloodsucker'. By now I have become so tired of permits, I'm willing to have my blood sucked. We let it be for now. The lawyer later turns out to represent the Thai Animal Protection Agency as well, the one threatening to end *Bring the elephant home*. Not just a bloodsucker, but a spy to boot.

At the office, Lee and I tackle maps and schedules. Our starting point will be Surin, the city where the annual elephant festival takes place in November. That's where we should buy our elephants, Lek says. 'There will be over three hundred elephants, and plenty of trade. You'll see the animals that wander around the cities for most of the year.' Lek joins us, her experience is essential. Marjolein of Nature Conservation Films and I agree to begin filming at the festival.

After the purchase, 'our' elephants will have time to recuperate in Surin. Somewhere nice, with lots of food and water, they will be able to get to know each other and their mahouts. In the meantime, I will travel back to Chiang Mai with the film crew, to film extensively at the Elephant Nature Park and in Elephant Haven. Afterwards my friend Hanna will come over from Holland, we'll assemble the team for the tour, and Lee, Hanna, and I will explore the route by car. In late December the whole team will celebrate Christmas with the elephants; then in early January we'll take off.

We will transport our freed elephants by truck to Ayutthaya, the starting point of our trek. Lee says we'll probably have to use the truck more often. There aren't always nature reserves to walk through, and not enough good places to rest. 'Safety first for our elephants,' he says. On the map, we locate the checkpoints where animal transports have to show their permits. We calculate distances and time periods. On average, an elephant in the wild can easily walk twenty kilometres a day. We decide to stick to ten a day, to be on the safe side, and have time for rest and relaxation. We arrive at an itinerary of two months, during which we won't have to hurry and will have plenty of time to relax.

For the transportation of goods and food along the way, we plan to use a mini-van from Lek's travel agency. Our driver will be Yut, a chubby, cheerful young man who has been working for Lek for years. He asks if his girlfriend Nong can come too, to cook. That seems to be a good idea, taking into account my abilities with a mortar. The miracles of Thai cuisine are not easily mastered, and we do need to feed about eight people three times a day: Lee, two mahouts, Yut, Nong, a vet, Hanna, and myself. And the driver of a truck every now and then.

***

Doi Suthep is a sacred mountain to the west of Chiang Mai. On the high crag overlooking the city glimmers a famous pilgrim temple. According to legend, in the fourteenth century King Kue Na released a white elephant with a relic of the Buddha on his back. The elephant was to indicate the spot where the relic was to be kept. After some diversions, the elephant climbed to this high spur near the summit of Doi Suthep. There he trumpeted three times, turned round three times, knelt down and died from exhaustion. King Kue Na built a temple on the spot.

At the foot of the stairs leading to the present-day temple is a male elephant, but this one is alive. If you can call it living. He stands on a bare concrete floor on a foot-long chain. For ten baht you can give him three pieces of bamboo. He never stops shaking his head and responds aggressively to the people in front of him. He strains at the chain around his leg, causing it to hang in the air all the time. His nails are broken from the concrete. He has no protection from the sun, no water, no other elephants near, no greens within trunk reach. Some Americans are shouting at the elephant. 'Ask the guy to let him play the harmonica, it's awesome!' one of them says to me. A Thai spectator pulls the trunk hard, for fun. The elephant has wounds on his head. He's from Surin, a province in the northeast. He's been here for about three months, because the owner can't provide for him in his own village anymore. Should I raise the matter with the temple monks? If they say it's illegal, it will be soon over. But where should this elephant go? At least he has food here, and the mahout makes some money. I pass it on to Lek. Perhaps later we can buy this elephant, too. I record a few words about him on the website.

One night sometime later I'm riding my scooter on the superhighway, a motorway south of Chiang Mai. There, underneath the fly-overs raised on pillars, on dark fields, possibly near rubbish dumps, is the most likely place to find street elephants, according to Lek. I want to see and record as much of their existence as possible. I drive around for two hours and get lost. Elephants seem to be everywhere, but when I get closer, they turn out to be rubbish piles, or shadows of rubbish piles. I keep an eye out for dung, or a truck with elephant food. I even try to smell them, but my nose is filled with exhaust fumes. I have a headache and my back starts to hurt from the scooter. I feel ridiculous. Do I really think I will find an elephant here? Riding around in circles on the motorway really doesn't make any sense. I go faster and faster and am angry with myself. Suddenly I spot an elephant in the busy traffic underneath the superhighway. Or is it? I stop on the spot, forgetting I'm on the superhighway, and hear screaming brakes behind me. The next exit turns out to be one-way, in the wrong direction. I try to ride back on the verge, but it's too dangerous so I ditch the scooter, and run back to the place where I had seen the elephant. He's about five years old, a plastic bag tied to his tail as a reflector, and bags of bananas on his back. I take pictures. The mahout and the woman selling fruit are happy to see a tourist. 'You want elephant ride?' I am stunned, here on the verge? '*Mop long*,' the mahout orders, 'On your stomach', and in the blink of an eye the elephant is down. I quietly offer the animal my apologies and promise to do everything in my power to help street elephants. I swear to him that one day he'll be back in the wild, with other elephants. Riding back afterwards, I get lost again.

***

My confidence in the project is mainly based on karma, the Buddhist notion that everything you do, say, and think will eventually come back to you. What goes around comes around, as we would say. You reap what you sow. In short, I just can't imagine anyone would want to prevent me from saving elephants. Setbacks are part of the deal, but surely the elephant gods are on my side?

The richest elephant karma I ever experienced was in 2003. Before going back to Holland to get *Bring the elephant home* off the ground, I wanted to travel through Laos. It's old name was Lan Xang, land of a million elephants! I leave almost all my cash, 250 euros, for the Park and arrive in Luang Prabang, the former capital of Laos, with 500 baht—ten euros. I locate a beautiful guesthouse on the Mekong River, and go and look for a cash point. People look at me in surprise. Cash point? The bank employees would be happy to slide *kips* across the counter for a credit card or traveller's check, but those I don't have. Perhaps there's one in Vientiane, the present capital. First, though, let's do the things I had planned to do, like watching the sun set from the temple high on a mountain above the city. On the climb, a young monk joins me. His name is Sith, he's sixteen years old, and he shows me where he eats and studies. He leads me to a famous footprint of the Buddha and to a place where you can 'make merit'. We burn incense, light candles, and throw lucky sticks, a form of fortunetelling. Then we watch the sunset. The vista around us turns into a magical orange realm through which the Mekong sparkles. I tell him about the elephants, about my dream. He tells me about his dream: to speak English well, and be a good person. 'When you act with your heart, in the end good will come to you. It always comes back!' I tell him I am without cash. 'Don't worry! If your money is with the elephants, you will have no problems! You don't need money, you need karma!' We laugh a lot and I give him the one hundred baht for the English textbook he needs. 'That may just be the extra karma you need!' Sith says.

Cheap street food and water: fifty baht. I consider my options. Could I get money at the bank with my father's credit card number? Western Union? Hook a tourist? Find a job? Sell my belongings? Live at the temple? None of it is realistic. Again somebody mentions the cash point in Vientiane. I buy a ticket for 120 baht and use my last coins for water and a bun. Twelve hours on the bus; the beautiful Lao landscape passes me by unnoticed because there's a cash point floating before my eyes. In one train of thought money comes out, in another it doesn't. We stop for lunch, but I stay on the bus. Even my water is almost gone. I arrive in Vientiane sick to my stomach with hunger. I strap on my backpack and walk. 'Where are you going?' a British lady asks. 'It takes over an hour to walk to the city and a *tuktuk* is only fifty baht.' 'I'm on my way to the cash point.' 'There isn't one.' She stops a *tuktuk* and pays the driver to take me into town. There's a cash point at the bank. I put in my card. No money. It's starting to get dark, there's nowhere to go, I'm hungry, the *tuktuk* driver wants more money. Two bank employees walk through the door and see my desperation. 'Laos is not connected to the cash point network. Don't you know anyone in Vientiane?' No, I just want to get out of this country as soon as possible! One of them gives the driver money and tells him to take me to the bridge over the Mekong. Across the bridge is Thailand. I don't know how to thank them. The driver races to the bridge. A luxury coach is waiting on the other side, going to Bangkok. 'Sorry, no money, can I please come?' 'No problem, sit here!' All I can think of is food. We stop at a restaurant. 'Free food for you, my friend, eat what you like.' The ticket collector takes me to a cash point on a motorbike and I buy crisps and drinks for everyone on the bus. How I love this country!

Ever since that trip I practice 'making merit' with total abandon. The Loi Krathong festival, just before we leave for Surin, is a good time for it. It takes place on a full moon in the Thai twelfth lunar month, usually November. '*Loi*' means 'to float', and a '*krathong*' is a small raft, traditionally made from a piece of banana tree, but nowadays often from foam or plastic. It's decorated with candles and flowers, incense and nicely folded leaves, and you float it down the river to honour Mae Phra Khongkha—Mother Ganges—the goddess of all waters. With the raft, you also let go of all your anger and resentment, to face life refreshed.

I buy a big white paper lantern which, propelled by a fire in a tray underneath, quickly and quietly takes to the air. On the bank of the Ping River, Pom and I fold our hands, bow, and launch our *krathong* on the current. The river looks magical with all those lights. A few hundred metres downstream a blockage forms, but our *krathong* floats around it. 'That is the power of your project,' Pom says. Would that be the way? Go with the flow and just steer clear of the obstacles? I look up at the sky, studded with lanterns. Could the highest one be mine, and if so, isn't success then more dependent on fiery zeal? Maybe the *krathong* strategy is better, to begin with. The lantern strategy is always a second option.

There's more merit to be made in the warm night. For a few baht, you can buy a cage with two birds, for you to release. According to the faces of the people who watch 'their' birds off, it has to be a wonderful feeling. But isn't this shallow and hypocritical, these critters have to be caught first, don't they? I don't think the elephant gods would approve.

In the river, a boy is fishing the *krathong* out of the water. He takes the money some people have put in, then lets the raft float off. A fat Dutch man yells: 'Take your paws of my *krathong*!' Leave the poor kid alone, I think, with the proverb in mind that I once read: 'Everybody acts on his own luck.' Pom gives the little fisherman some money and tells him he had better go a little further downstream.

***

One week before departure. Six weeks after my arrival we haven't gotten anywhere yet with regard to the permits. Lek announces we're about to meet the princess and the Prime Minister, but I'm not sure anymore it will actually happen. She constantly runs in and out of the office, does one interview after another, has to leave for Taiwan soon to receive the Hero of Asia award, all great for the elephants but she has hardly spent any time on *Bring the elephant home*.

41

The princess can't receive us after all because she's not well. As we learn, we won't be meeting the Prime Minister now either, so we pin our hopes on the Minister of the Environment, who will be in Chiang Mai this week. Lek knows a journalist who is in touch with him. She sends our plan to the Minister's office; the journalist will check up on it. Every day I buttonhole him: 'Well?' 'No, nothing yet . . .' Then Lek suddenly loses it over the government's plan to export Thai elephants to Australia, and takes the Environmental Minister to court. The man who is supposed to help us get the permits.

I chuck my wrinkly black silk dress in the dustbin.

A bout of migraine tells me I hardly believe in a happy ending anymore, no matter how often I tell everybody else that I do. Haven't had one in a long time, a migraine attack. The last one was during my short commercial career. When Lek talks about the walk, I feel like doing it, but I dread Surin, where the Nature Conservation Films crew is waiting to film the purchase of the elephants. How am I supposed to do this under these circumstances? How can I talk about the project with confidence when everything is sliding? I try to keep my spirits up. The benefit festival was about to fail as well, but I managed to bluff my way through, didn't I? After tomorrow, my time in Chiang Mai is over, so I will only have people around me who believe in the plan. We'll see where we end up. Come on, Antoinette, you've been in tighter spots. It's just that I can't recall when.

Pom is worried about me. Just leave me alone a bit, I say over the phone, but she's already at my door. In her pick-up truck, we take a drive through Chiang Mai. I buy some fruit, she buys grilled crickets, a local delicacy, which she cracks between her teeth. We sit down on a couple of parked scooters. I bring up my insecurities and my frustrations. Pom tells me Lek is willing to do everything for my project. How often hasn't she said she's happy with my help, that she likes the way we work together. 'Then why doesn't she help me more? Why doesn't she get the permits for me?' All my frustrations of the past weeks pour out and I burst into tears. 'I am sick and tired of this project! I wish I had never started this. You should have warned me!' Pom is distraught, she has never seen me this way. She tells me she has always had faith in me. Of course she has worried and felt responsible; we came up with the plan together, didn't we? 'But this is all part of it, this is Thailand! I told you, you should have come here three months ago, your schedule was too tight. But everything will be all right, you have the right attitude and I'm on your side.' 'Yes, but you don't take care of the permits either,' I say, still blubbering a bit. 'Don't worry so much, don't be so weak. And please show your happy face again, it makes you beautiful.' In protest I walk home, wearing my ugliest face and stamping my feet. Eventually, though, I can laugh about it, too.

My final day in Chiang Mai. Or aren't we going to Surin tonight? In the morning I meet Lek at the office and tell her we have to talk. 'Nothing we absolutely need has been arranged. No Minister, no princess, no lawyer, no permits. I'm worried. I wish you had tried harder to get the permits.' Lek is taken aback by my directness and apologises. 'The media have taken up all my time, I'm sorry. But I do have faith in it.' I feel like saying 'We can't buy elephants this way.' But there will be a film crew waiting tomorrow, and nowhere will we find as many elephants together as at the festival. So I say: 'We should have had the permits a long time ago. Should I go to Surin?' 'Don't worry. We'll have another month after the festival, won't we? Everything will be okay.'

As always, it remains unclear what time we are going to leave, whether there's a van, and who will be going along. Lee calls: departure is at eight o'clock p.m. from the office. I have to clear out my apartment, pack my bags, and turn in my rented scooter. I can leave my belongings at the office. With time to spare, I get on the scooter. Bags on my back, between my feet, on the handlebars, in the basket up front. I ride towards the river and find the bridge closed. Next bridge, closed; next bridge, closed; next bridge . . . now I'm riding along the ring road around Chiang Mai. On the final night of Loi Krathong, it is impossible to cross the river. I get lost, get stuck in traffic, fireworks explode around me. I call the office to let them know that I will be late. Lee hears that I'm lost and calls me. He drives through the chaos of the traffic to come and find me. Driving ahead of the scooter he tries to find a way through, but every road that is not closed off leads out of town. We finally arrive at the office an hour late.

4

Revolutions

THE PETCHKASEM HOTEL seems a mite too large for the provincial capital of Surin in eastern Thailand. Among the shops selling spare parts and office supplies, the grand staircase leading to the golden entrance seems a bit over the top. The white concrete building towers over the narrow streets. In the square in front of the hotel, elephants stand neatly lined up in the parking spots for cars. They have howdahs on their backs and the mahouts are doing their very best to persuade the Petchkasem guests to take a seat.

Today is the start of the forty-fifth Elephant Round-up of Surin, a two-day festival where hundreds of elephants are brought together to show off their tricks. 'The elephant is part of the national identity of Thailand,' the governor of Surin writes in the programme. 'Surin has the largest number of domesticated elephants in the country. The elephants and the people of Surin have a long-time connection of love and understanding. The elephants are considered to be family.'

It is mainly the Suai, also called Kui, who keep elephants here. They are a tribe that has moved here from Laos. They used to hunt elephants in the wild, mainly in Laos and Cambodia where forests were less ravaged than in Thailand. When Laos and Cambodia got involved in the Vietnam War in the 1970s, such hunts almost came to an end. Since 1989, wild elephants are officially an endangered species, and hunting has been completely banned. Still there are always rumours about animals being caught illegally.

The Suai have domesticated and trained elephants for centuries. In ancient chronicles, tribal members were said to be exempt from military service because they provided elephants for the army. If these survived the war, they were allowed to go back to Surin to enjoy their retirement. This is even mentioned as the origin of the existence of 'house' elephants. Surin had plenty of forests in those days, and the animals were also used for peaceful purposes, such as building temples. On the other hand, I have also read that the Suai are opposed to using elephants for forestry and other heavy labour. 'They live side by side with elephants, as friends or sons.' So the animal is a son, but they will send him to war. He hauls bricks for temples, but logs from the forest are too heavy. He is sacred, but his will has to be broken in training. Will I ever understand?

At the crack of dawn, a long parade of elephants head for the festival grounds. Mahouts bob astride their necks, goads held loosely in their hands. One little mahout can't be more than twelve years old. Some are grey and stiff. Most of them are young gods on their high thrones. If an elephant pulls a little to the side, he gets a tap with the hook on the left or the right and obediently falls back in line. A herd of stampeding elephants can make the earth thunder, but this crowd sounds like a group of old men in slippers. Elephants have thick callused foot soles, and they dearly need them because of their huge weight. Shh shh shh go the callused feet on the asphalt. A strolling elephant can hardly be heard.

One of the animals draws my attention from afar because of a large stain on his forehead. Blood? No, I guess not. It's a purple disinfectant used to treat wounds. The forehead is a mess, more pink than grey from all the scars made by the hooked goad. Many of the elephants have scars like that. And some of the young gods wear shabby old clothes. Poor buggers on top of poor buggers.

The first elephant I see on the festival grounds is a skinny female that rocks back and forth, leaning over on a chain between her front legs. Her right hind leg is deformed. The woman owner, selling little bags of sugar cane, tells me her name is Malai Thong and that she is for sale. She wants 180,000 baht, 3,600 euros. 'Take it!' my heart calls out. But how can I ask a cripple elephant to walk to Chiang Mai?

The owner says that her family bought the elephant three years ago. 'On the job in the logging industry she stepped on a landmine. She was young, we wanted to raise her, and we thought that leg would heal. Now our money is gone and she can't work, so we have to sell her.' Apparently I am not the only one to come to the festival for other reasons than to watch elephants painting or playing tug-of-war. Because, today, that's what they do. When the stands surrounding the oval stadium field have filled up—there's a separate part for foreign visitors, where an English speaker explains the proceedings—the opening music starts. Majestic tunes herald the stadium-wide arrival of hundreds of elephants—a thoroughly impressive sight. You can understand why armies used to run when a force like this appeared on the battlefield. Only when the elephants come closer can you see some very sad ones among them, with dull eyes, protruding ribs, and a hide covered with scars.

Throughout the festival, contradictory feelings bombard me. It's extraordinary how elephants carefully step over and between the people who have lain down crossways in a long line in the grass. But do they really have to bow for the applause like Disney's Dumbo? It's unbelievable how an elephant can pull along eighty grown men. But I've seen on film how much violence is used in logging to force an elephant to do heavy labour. Having elephants paint T-shirts is just stupid. Besides, Lek tells me the brush only goes up and down because in the training the top and the bottom of the trunk are being poked alternately. Elephants playing soccer? I'd prefer even to go and see our national football team.

The radiant, dancing Suai boys and girls cheer me up, but my mood sinks again at the fake war. Agile swordfighters jump around the field like fleas, fireworks explode, splendidly decorated elephants walk through the smoke and thunder. Hard training must have preceded all this. There's a reason villagers use fireworks to chase off elephants that raid their plantations, they hate this kind of loud noise. And in real wars, elephant vanguards have on occasion turned back in panic, to trample their own armies. An elephant doesn't want to make war. I think of something a Thai friend once said: 'It's because of the elephants the kingdom of Siam survived!', putting his hand over his heart. The audience is the same, it displays a mixture of pride and admiration, maybe even love. When, at the end of the day, the mahouts parade their animals along the stands, plenty of banknotes are held out to the trunks to pass up and back over to the mahouts.

***

From behind a pond at the back of the festival grounds, a young elephant comes running toward me, screaming. With panic in her eyes, she comes to a halt right in front of me. She feels cold, she's shivering. She can't be more than six years old, although her face is that of a sixty-year-old. Instead of playful and wayward, she is fearful and tense. Her forehead especially shows signs of having been lacerated with the hooked goad. Her ears are infected, her nails are dry, she is skinny. When I put my hands on her face, she gives me a penetrating gaze. Her breathing is agitated. It's like she is silently crying for help. To me it is love at first sight. The mahout says her name is Dok-ngeon. 'Silver Flower', Lee translates. She is from Surin and has been begging in Pattaya, the beach spa south of Bangkok. Now she is back in Surin to get further training. She has mastered the basic techniques, but her mahout wants to teach her some special tricks. She is not part of the festival at all, so why is she here? To be sold, Lee says. Besides, owners receive over two hundred euros from the organisation if they bring their elephant here, and half of the transportation expenses.

The next day, Dok-ngeon is standing in full sunlight on a short chain. She is walking in circles. At one stage, she picks up the chain with her trunk and drops it in front of my feet. Unchain me! Yesterday she was panicky and hurt, today she's angry. I silently promise her a better life and ask Lee to open negotiations. The mahout wants 350,000 baht, 7,000 euros. That is a lot by current market prices. My Western passport has many advantages, but it is bad for our bargaining position. I agree with the mahout to visit him at his village the day after the festival.

That afternoon at least ten mahouts check in with Lee. They all want to sell their elephants. Lee drags me along from one to another. Another one missing a foot, two babies covered with wounds, a blind female, one that for some unknown reason is very cheap. I ask questions, hear stories, and begin getting confused. The cameraman and soundman from the film crew follow us relentlessly. A little circus elephant makes ten bows for me. 'What do you think, you want to buy this one?' Lee keeps asking me. I don't want to make any decisions while caught up in this madness. It makes me sad. Walking around like this to buy an elephant is ridiculous. It was never my intention to get involved in the elephant trade! The terrifying thought occurs to me that two new elephants might be taken from the wild to replace the ones I am buying. It happens sometimes, Lee says. To some mahouts, elephants are no more than commodities. They buy a young elephant in Burma, Laos or Cambodia, bring it up, then sell it.

At least one elephant is freed today. For over two thousand euros, Lek buys Malai Thong, the female who had stepped on a landmine. She just stands there swaying back and forth, not yet realising how lucky she is.

Part of the festival's revenue goes to an elephant hospital in Surin. We decide to go and visit this. Or rather, we barge in with two film crews. Lek is followed by a camera for Italian television, and the Animal Planet crew follows me. At the hospital, we also find a South Korea television crew that is using the festival to promote a national pop star. Or the other way around, it isn't quite clear. The pop star looks tired. She couldn't care less about the sick elephants.

Lek though immediately connects with them, she looks in ears and mouths, murmurs consolations. A small and a large elephant stand in an enclosure. The little one has a broken leg. When he and his mahout were hit by a car in the streets of Bangkok, he managed to drag the mahout to the side of the road. He is a hero, says Lek. The big elephant has eaten garbage in Bangkok and has been throwing up for a week. While she is eating, a green liquid is constantly oozing from her mouth. The owner suddenly says that I can take her for 7,500 euros. It makes me sick.

On our way back, my mood sinks even deeper when Lek tells me about the press conference given yesterday by the Thai Animal Protection Agency. They told the press that during the trek I will walk the freed elephants on asphalt all day. Apparently Lee has been scolded as well, by the governor of Surin province no less. We decide to hold an emergency meeting, tonight in the hotel lobby.

At the end of the afternoon, a beautiful elephant is waiting in front of the hotel for tourists to ride on her back. Her name is Si-nuan. Lee translates: 'Soft colour, sexy girl, hundred percent lady.' Suddenly he starts to sing and move his arms gracefully. 'It is the name of a classic Thai song!'

She has large ears, a clear-cut pigmentation pattern, a full tail. 'Suai!' the mahout lisps, 'pretty!' He behaves rather like a pimp recommending a favourite girl from his stables. I feed her some cucumbers, which she eats slowly. 'Are her teeth all right?' I ask the mahout, whose name is Wichian. 'Very much okay,' he says, 'she's just a very slow elephant.' According to him, Si-nuan is thirty-five; I think she looks at least ten years older. She is from Phrae, a province on the borders with Burma, where she used to work in a show. One night she broke free from her chain and took off. When she was eating in a plantation, someone took a shot at her with a catapult, and hit her in the eye. Wichian bought her two years ago, to take her begging. It must be scary to hear the traffic whiz by when you're blind on one side. I feed her some more cucumbers, pet her trunk, and think: we'll just have to buy you.

Wichian wants six thousand euros. He tells me Si-nuan has a daughter, Nung Ning. When she was eight months old, he sold her to an elephant show in Phuket, a year and a half ago.

An idea springs to mind immediately. What if we could find Nung Ning, reunite her with Si-nuan and take them to the Elephant Nature Park together? It doesn't take me long to decide.

At seven o'clock, we assemble for the emergency meeting. It is an uneasy conversation, and that's not just because of the decibel storm from the karaoke stage in the dining room. Lek is giving in a bit to the pressure from the opponents of my project. 'Can I go on?' I ask. 'You can do the walk,' Lek says. 'Only if you support me, and only if it is the right thing for the elephants and for the Elephant Nature Park,' I answer. 'It is not good to walk on the roads,' says Lek. I protest: 'That's not what we're going to do, is it? Aren't we walking through nature reserves?'

Suddenly that appears to be much harder than before. Lee starts talking about roads and cities, rice fields, and plantations. Lek explains that the British people who made an attempt earlier, had to walk on asphalt, too. I wish I had known this before. But I'm not really surprised, though. On the train from Bangkok to Chiang Mai, I had been viewing the landscape with increasing alarm. Rice fields as far as the eye can see. No forests, forests only begin up north. The northeast, where we are now, is even more tree-less. The anxiety that had come over me in the past few months, becomes acute. Not a single permit has been arranged, no audience with the princess, and the Thai animal protectors could be right. Maybe the route is unsuitable for walking. 'What is our biggest problem?' I ask. 'It's not the permits,' Lek says. 'It's public opinion.' Then I spring the plan on them to find Nung Ning, Si-nuan's daughter. The idea to reunite them goes down well, even though Lek has concerns about fitting in all three elephants in the herd.

Feverishly, I think of what to do next. Under no circumstance will I walk them on asphalt. We need a plan B. In fact, the only possibility is to move the elephants by truck. But we don't have to give up the entire trip, do we? We can make camp at temples and visit schools just as we had planned, keep the publicity wheels turning. Right? 'Better,' Lee says, relieved. So he has had doubts in his mind the whole time. We agree that Lee and I will visit the owners of Dok-ngeon and Si-nuan in their villages tomorrow, and go to the district animal offices to take care of the paperwork. After that, we'll take off for Phuket to find Nung Ning.

We celebrate the end of the festival with a beer at the bar. Chang beer, of course. Behind us a big white man splashes around in the hotel pool. 'There's an elephant in the pool,' someone says. My heart skips a beat. Of course, a unique attraction, swimming with an elephant! Thank God, it was only a joke about the fat man; I'm clearly close to losing my mind! On the karaoke stage, heavily painted ladies sing on, despite the fact that there is no one left in the room. Slowly, I let the idea sink in, that the walk has been cancelled. In just one day, the scenario I have had in mind for a year and a half, has been discarded. After weeks of waiting, of questions without answers, of lonely toiling, suddenly everything is happening at once. Upstairs in my hotel room, I try to make a start on a report of the festival to put on the website. I stare at the blank screen and wonder where in heaven's name I should begin. Later, I slide into an uneasy sleep and dream of a festival where a large herd of elephants is running amok.

***

On our way to Si-nuan's village, it becomes clear why elephants can't live here anymore. There is no forest left, not even a shrub. The only trees growing here in groups are plantation trees: banana, eucalyptus, papaya, while in the fields grow cassava and rice. Harvest has just passed, the rice grains have been left to dry out along the sides of the road spread over large blue canvases, sometimes so much heaped up that there's only one lane left for traffic.

Si-nuan has a day off. Together with the village cows and some other elephants, she is peacefully gleaning the stubble of a harvested rice field. Wichian, the mahout, and his family live in the most luxurious house in the village. We sit down on the wooden veranda in front of the house and start negotiations, while the film crew keeps orbiting us once again. No wonder the entire village turns out to look on in amazement. Children peek around the corner, and when I look at them they bolt with a giggle.

The family grows rice, Wichian says. When the harvest is over, they go and beg with the elephants. They visit all the cities in the northeast of Thailand: Nong Khai, Nakhon Phanom, Roi Et, Udon Thani, and Si Sa Ket. We try to find out more about Si-nuan and Nung Ning but soon get bogged down in obscurities. Age, purchase dates, selling dates; in Wichian's story everything keeps changing. We check the available paperwork. Every elephant's name, old and new owner, and the price have to be written down in an owner's document. Si-nuan's papers seem to check out. She was bought along with Nung

Ning and brought to Surin. In the transportation documents, both elephants are mentioned. In that of Nung Ning, there's a sales document that says she is in Phuket. 'She's the star of a show down there!' Wichian says, falling back into his role of pimp.

The price for Si-nuan is not negotiable. 'That's the way we are around here. Once we've named a price, we stick to it. Even if you were to offer more, I would still say no.' We decide to leave it at that. We have copies made of the documents, so we can have them checked at the district animal office.

The visit to Dok-ngeon's mahout is a bizarre story. At nightfall, we arrive at a dusty village. Nobody in sight, although somewhere music is blaring so loudly that I wouldn't be surprised if the villagers had all fled. After some looking about, we find the given address, a bar under a thatched roof. The mahout isn't home, so we phone him, to hear he's on his way. We order a beer from the barmaid, the mahout's sister. According to her, Dok-ngeon is presently being trained at a camp sponsored by Thai Airlines. Then the mahout arrives in a beautiful car, the woman at his side is draped in ivory jewellery. He says Dok-ngeon needs another week of training. She has to learn to play the harmonica. Can we go and see her tomorrow? Oh yes, no problem.

Dok-ngeon, he says, was bought only a month ago, at a village near the Burmese border. A month ago? Hadn't she worked in Pattaya? No, that's not true. Documents appear. Dok-ngeon turns out to have an implanted microchip, a means of identification that nowadays is inserted under the skin, and is mandatory by Thai law. The accompanying registration document also describes administered medication. Huh? Botox? No joke, 2 cc of Botox. We think of poor, wrinkly Dok-ngeon and get the giggles. But we need to negotiate seriously. Eight thousand euros, the mahout says. That's a thousand more than at the festival. Casually he adds he might take her back to Pattaya. He looks at me with an arrogant gaze. 'He is not the owner,' Lee says. 'It's obvious this kid gets a commission. We have to talk to the real owner.'

Tired and disappointed, we drive back to Surin. Nothing accomplished, and a whole lot of uncertainties to deal with. Actually, it is not surprising. There is so much illegality where elephants are concerned: the begging, the training, the trade. I am overcome with doubt. Will Nung Ning even be in Phuket? Shouldn't I have bought Si-nuan and Dok-ngeon immediately?

In the car to Surin, I try to dispel my disappointment with thoughts of the Park. Maybe Si-nuan can become friends with Lilly, she's a slow one, too. Lilly has recently been disappointed in friendship. Mae Keao is a female elephant, found in bad health on a Jumbo Express trip. An American woman, who had joined the Express, paid for her. Mae Keao has a rather dominant character. Mae Keao and Lilly became friends. Until a mother with a baby arrived at the Park. Then Mae Keao, that twister, bit Lilly's tail and buttered up the mother— who turned her down in the end, which I thought was rather sad. Lilly, with her sore tail, still follows Mae Keao around every now and then.

By now, there are so many old ladies at the Park that a special house has been built for them. When it is cold at night, the mahouts build a fire for them. Mae Bia is the most recent arrival. According to her documents, she was eighty-five when she was brought to the Park from a trekking camp in Chiang Rai in October of 2005. She was skinny, had lots of infected wounds, and was shy. She used to work in the logging industry; fifteen years ago she was sold to the trekking business. Now that she was unable even to carry tourists, the owner wanted to sell her. Fortunately, two Brits were willing to pay. When we were about to load Mae Bia into the truck, the owner's wife started to cry. She was aware of the good life her elephant would get at Lek's, but she did have difficulty in letting her go. While I was driving behind the truck, my heart suddenly skipped a beat. 'Not too long now, and I will be driving behind our own elephants', I thought. When Mae Bia arrived at the Park, she ambled straight to the meadow and started to eat, going on till she was ready to burst. Her mahout fed her nice snacks all day. Sticky rice with peeled bananas, tamarind with salt—real haute cuisine. For quite some time, she kept aloof from the herd. Hope, the six-year-old teenager, couldn't accept this. But he was tactful about it. Usually he is boisterous, but this time he approached carefully and lightly touched Mae Bia with his trunk. She allowed him more and more liberties, till from a certain moment on, Mae Bia was bathing with the other elderly ladies. Today she is part of the herd, even though she is still shy and occasionally prefers to snooze in the shade of a tree.

How would Dok-ngeon fare? She's only a little older than Hope and Jungle Boy. In my dreams, she is the girl at the centre of their attention. With Si-nuan in the background, as a foster mom, keeping her on the straight and narrow.

***

The animal registration office is a little outside of town, surrounded by fields full of hay. In the hallway of the small rundown building, there are posters about chicken batteries that look just like the ones back home. There's also one about cock fighting with the title *Fighting Cock Passport*. From behind the building, a sleepy man appears. Aha, elephants? He calls the boss. He shows up after a while, disappears into the office without saying a word and sits behind an empty desk for fifteen minutes. Only then can we come in. He doesn't even deign to look at me. A 2002 calendar hangs on the wall behind him. Lee explains that we would like to verify Si-nuan's and Nung Ning's papers.

This official is a gifted actor. Looking bored, he fishes a file out of the left hand desk drawer. He thumbs through it, sighs, pushes his glasses a little higher on his nose. He rummages in the right hand drawer, another file. Thumbing, sighing. 'We'll be organising a big agricultural show in a while,' he finally tells Lee. 'Can't this foreign woman come and sit on a tractor? It was a huge success at the last show! We must be friends first. Maybe then I can do something for you.'

On our way to the animal office where Dok-ngeon's documents are said to be kept, we suddenly spot Si-nuan's mahout Wichian behind us on a motorbike. At the office, he tries to keep us from going in; he says he'll take care of everything himself. When we nevertheless march into the office, draw a number and sit down, he joins us. We wait. But since we're here . . .'I bid 250,000 baht for Si-nuan,' I say. Five thousand three hundred euros, seven hundred less than his asking price. Wichian turns out to be a gifted actor as well. The corners of his mouth turn down, he looks up at the sky in despair. He definitely won't go below 300,000. How about 275,000? He borrows a pen, writes on his hand: 299,000. Twenty euros down; I don't believe I'm a credit to the Dutch business spirit. 'You are rich!' Wichian whispers, giving me a flirtatious look. 'Rich and beautiful!' We're not getting anywhere. Then it turns out he is at the office to buy an elephant himself. 'For how much?' I ask. Three hundred fifty thousand baht. 'You are rich yourself!' I say. He asks about Dok-ngeon, how much does she cost? 380,000 baht? Far too much for such an unreliable elephant. She's gone back in training for a reason, as she's impossible to work with. Now take Si-nuan!

After forty-five minutes, we're next. This time the official is responsive. Sure enough, Dok-ngeon's mahout isn't her owner. 'Commission man,' Lee says. The name Dok-ngeon turns out to be new, she used to be called Mae Lai. 'Miss

Wrinkle,' Lee says. A name well chosen. We find out who the owner is and where he lives, and rush off. The village is situated on a tributary of the Moon River, which in turn is a tributary of the Mekong River. It is surrounded by rice fields and eucalyptus plantations. The men of the village are drunk, they hang about apathetically and laugh at everything and nothing. Dok-ngeon's owner is drunk too. 'My wife is ill,' he mumbles. 'We have no money anymore to provide for Dok-ngeon.' Instead of 8,000 euros, he now asks almost 9,000. I offer him 6,400. He promises to talk it over with the family. We should feel free to go and see Dok-ngeon, she's not at a training camp but in a field nearby.

I recognise her from afar. She's chained up, but the place she's in doesn't look too bad, a harvested rice field with plenty of water and a little shade from eucalyptus trees. She comes to me, with blood on her ears and her face. Furthermore, there are sharp wooden pins inserted between her ears and neck, invisible to the outside world. These are used in training, to teach an elephant on the road not to graze on trees and shrubbery left and right. When I greet her, she is unable to move her head. So, she is in training after all.

I am on her territory now. I have inspected her, now it's her turn to check me out. I sit down on a rock and stay there unmoving. Cautiously she comes over to investigate. Closer and closer, sniffing deeply through her trunk. When I reach to put my hand on it, she pulls back: 'Don't touch me, it's my turn now,' I take this to mean. She comes and stands right beside me, her mouth open wide. I leave her to do her own thing. I trust her and hope she is beginning to trust me, too.

That night I worry. Why didn't we bring her some bananas? Shouldn't I have turned around those wooden pins secretly? Then she could have spent the afternoon without pain. But we also would have lost the mahout's trust, and perhaps the chance of buying her. I take comfort in the thought that in a little while we will be able to offer her a better life, no matter what. I'm determined to get Dok-ngeon free in December.

***

The only way to find Nung Ning is to actually go to Phuket. With copies of her sales documents in hand, we first travel to Bangkok. After all those complications, we have to take stock, put things in writing, and look at film material. The mini-van functions as a mobile office. Data from cameras are uploaded to mobile hard disks, CDs burnt, laptops worked hard, telephones keep ringing, as the website is updated.

When we enter the city, I stare out the window without seeing anything. My thoughts are chaotic. What if we can't find Nung Ning? I left Dok-ngeon behind in Surin while she was in training. Shouldn't I have bought her right away? Will Si-nuan be back on the streets tonight? Did I really shift my plans this weekend? All our supporters have sponsored an elephant journey on foot, but suddenly they are going to travel on wheels. Would they ask for their money back?

At a quarter to ten we stop at a guesthouse. Just in time for the monthly Dutch radio interview over the phone. What should I say? That we won't be walking? I really cannot explain the problem in ten minutes. When the connection has been made, I just talk about the festival and the two elephants we have chosen. After that, the e-mail has to be checked, as there won't be much time for that in Phuket. There are lots of messages from people who want to join the walk, especially from young girls. It makes me face facts. I really have to go public about cancelling the walk. There is one extraordinary e-mail. A man from St. Petersburg, Russia, has been so moved by the website message about the Doi Suthep temple elephant, that he is donating his savings to buy him.

Then Lek calls. In Chiang Mai, a business called the 'Night Safari' will open soon, a wildlife park where people can observe animals by night . . . and then eat them. Besides elephant, the menu will feature giraffe, tiger, lion, horse, kangaroo, crocodile, dog, and snake. All legal and imported fresh daily, the restaurant owner says. How crazy is that? Of course you shouldn't eat animals at all, but that the Thai can eat elephants is beyond me. Is the elephant their national pride or just an extra large steak? That, I would like to know. Some time ago there was a fuss about the export of eight elephants to an Australian zoo, as a solution to the lack of habitat in Thailand, but I guess eating them is another option. Fortunately, there will be a protest march, Lek will be on the barricades. Later it will appear that the public outcry caused the plan to be quietly abandoned.

Again I sleep little, as I keep worrying. What if Nung Ning is not a baby at a circus after all, but a thirty-year-old at someone's home? What if she has died, and someone is using her documents for an imported baby? I am dying to see what will happen when mother and child meet. We could see if it's true that elephants recognise their family after many years. What if there's no Nung

Ning to be found? I should meditate, as Lee does. 'I sit quietly and everything stops,' he says.

We have the next day to ourselves because we'll take the train south in the evening. We take a water taxi to Wat Pho Temple. Water taxi and temple are perfect to hide from traffic. At Wat Pho, the roar disappears only ten metres from the entrance. The main temple harbours a Buddha almost fifty metres long, lying on its side with mother-of-pearl soles to its feet. Unforgettable. Tourists and Thai shuffle past, dumbfounded together. The only sound is the clicking of cameras and the chink of coins in collection plates. In smaller temples nearby, people kneel in front of smaller Buddha statues, bowing their heads and praying.

During my course in anthropology, I visited Thailand in 2003 to do a survey among young Thai about 'making merit'. From the survey, I got the impression that, although young people aren't brought up anymore in the old communities with community values, they definitely still 'make merit'. The difference is that nowadays it comes from the heart, rather than from social values. Targets of good deeds have changed as well. Young people don't give money to monks anymore, but to Greenpeace. But Lee says young people are still religious. He talks about Khao Phansa, 'the time to come inside and meditate'. When the three-month-long rainy season begins, the monks retreat to the monasteries. People bring them money and food, and parents send their sons to the monasteries during this season. Therefore Thai youngsters still have Buddhism in their blood. Would they be susceptible to a campaign about better elephant lives? 'I think young people are quicker than older people to disapprove of working elephants to death,' Lee says.

Travelling through Thailand by train is wonderful. The seats are spacious, you don't have to contend with your opposite neighbour for leg space. In the daytime, the open window allows you to enjoy the landscape, alternating now and again with flowery train stations where there are always two men. The first one holds up a green or a red flag, the second one stands behind him with his hands behind his back. At night, a berth with real cotton sheets is made up for you, there is a nightlight to read by, and at intervals vendors come by with beer and water. While the train is swaying through the night, I sleep like a log.

The next morning, we tumble from the train into Surat Thani, a town that functions as a tourist relay station for the various holiday island resorts. While waiting for the bus to Phuket, I read a leaflet about FantaSea Cultural Theme

Park. 'The award-winning Las Vegas-style Production Spectacle, colourfully blending the beauty of Thai culture with magical illusions, 4-D effects, aerial ballet, acrobatics, pyrotechnics, special effects, exciting stunts, and an elephant circus featuring over thirty elephants.' If Nung Ning is the star here, she has gone a long way in her short life.

The Phuket animal office is a great help. All 185 elephants that earn a living for their owners are in a computer file, which we can check for ourselves. We focus on every name, every age, every owner, every time of arrival. With each column, my hopes disintegrate further, to end up in a pathetic little pile. There's no little elephant that could possibly be Nung Ning. The veterinarian manning the office says she has to be in this file if she has been sold legally in Phuket. Even if she has been resold or renamed. But there are also plenty of other elephants with illegal documents. Once captured in Burma, Laos, or Cambodia, they are supplied with the documents of elephants that have died or been sold abroad, for example, to zoos in Malaysia or Indonesia. Illegal traders often evade the law, adroitly concluding deals with corrupt authorities. But, the civil servant says, he loves his wife and child too much to meddle in this. 'It is mafia business, we're no match for that.'

It has started to rain softly. We look for the name of Nung Ning's owner in the phone book, in vain. What has happened to her? Has she been put on a ship in Phuket and sold to another country? Have her documents been used to move another baby elephant into Thailand? All we can do now is visit all the shows and trekking camps in Phuket, and talk to mahouts. They know a lot of elephants, and where they're from, so might remember Nung Ning's story. In a copy shop, Lee makes leaflets to hand out among the mahouts. 'Wanted: Pretty little elephant from Surin called Nung Ning. Age: two to three years old. Her mother is blind in one eye. Reward 500 baht. If anyone knows where she is, please call me.' And then his phone number.

We don't have much time. We have to go to the Elephant Nature Park in a few days, where the crew from Nature Conservation Films is waiting for us. We rent a *tuktuk* for a day. A poster on its side says 'Bavarian Oktoberfest, opening 10 December!' Through curtains of rain, we race to the coast, where almost all the shows and trekking camps are located. Between the flat centre of the island and the beaches lies a steep range of hills. Here the tsunami waves must have broken in 2004, leaving the city of Phuket unscathed. But when we whiz down from the top, the beaches look like nothing has happened there either. Here and there new hotels are being built, and a grassy dike has been raised. This was the first coastal stretch where rebuilding started. Understandable really, considering the numbers of tourists still coming in and the money to be made. We drive past an exclusive residential area under construction with a billboard saying: 'Some people call this paradise. You can call it home.'

The trekking camps are mainly on the coast. Some are better tended than others, sizes vary. In most of these camps, elephants do shows. They kneel, bow, stand on their hind legs, play the harmonica, the full package. You can also take a ride into the hills on their backs. 'The jungle', as it is called on the advertising signs. Okay, it's not the Amsterdam Vondelpark, but 'jungle' really is just too much.

The award-winning Las Vegas Production Spectacle is closed. And also totally enclosed, as the huge grounds are surrounded by a high wall and guarded as if it were a military compound. It won an award in 2002 as Thailand's best tourist attraction. It cost three million baht to build, while it employs a thousand people and thirty-nine elephants. A publicity spokesman says Nung Ning might be registered in Bangkok, at the Safari World theme park, to which FantaSea is affiliated. I call and speak to a friendly lady managing director. After listening to my scatterbrain story about wanting to find a baby elephant I fell in love with two years ago, the director says: 'You must really love elephants, just as we do. But we don't know Nung Ning. What are you going to do when you find her? You can't just keep her at your apartment?' My story does sound a little strange, I admit, and I blurt out the truth, about wanting to take Nung Ning back to her mother. But that doesn't make her materialise either.

Siam Safari, Elephant Treks, the Kinnaree Shooting Range, Island Safari, Bukit Safari—it is turning out to be a wet, hopeless journey past sad elephants. Nowhere do we find a two-and-a-half-year-old girl elephant with star qualities and a one-eyed mother in Surin.

At the Safari Elephant Club, we hear of a baby elephant on the beach of an expensive hotel. We pass by there as well. Our clothes and hairdos are a far cry from the five-star kind, nevertheless we float into Le Meridien over reflective floors among grovelling receptionists. Halfway across the immense lobby, a breathtakingly beautiful girl is singing a classical Thai song, accompanied by a breathtakingly beautiful boy. With two small hammers he beats on the strings of a horizontal sounding board. 'A *khim*,' Lee says. He seems to know everything about everything. It sounds fabulous, but no one is listening.

Past the bar, the pool, the bowling lawn, and the tennis court, we eventually arrive at the beach. It's dry outside, in between showers. There we find Jimjim, two-and-a-half, but not a girl. His mahout doesn't carry a hook since Jimjim doesn't have to perform silly tricks. He just has to be nice to the guests, who hardly even notice his presence. Not such a bad life, compared to his family members at the trekking camps.

The zoo—even writing about it is difficult. A beastly mess. At the end of the day, Lee has handed out all of the leaflets. We have given up hope of finding Nung Ning. There's only one person who can help us now: Wichian, Si-nuan's mahout. He knows who Nung Ning was sold to. In a last desperate effort, we call him. For money, he's willing to come over immediately.

***

Wichian knows FantaSea's mahout manager. On the phone, the latter allows that there is an elephant answering to Nung Ning's profile on the books, but it has a different name. He also knows a Nung Ning working on the beach of the Laguna Resort. We decide to check that one out first.

Laguna is a collection of villas, every one with its own swimming pool and staff. The guests are driven around the grounds in golf carts. They can also use the elephants, waiting for them near the entrance. Wichian talks to their mahouts. Are there any babies here? Certainly. My heart beats faster. They point in the direction of the mahout village, a little further on into the grounds. We climb a fence and end up between ramshackle huts made of corrugated iron, housing three mahout families. Three small elephants are standing on a slab of concrete. On entering one of the huts, we find two tiny rooms with mats on the floor, a hammock with a baby, and a television showing two Thai soap opera stars squabbling. Wichian gets a bottle of water and sits down. They're all mahouts together. Nung Ning? No, the pride of the family is called Ning Nong, six years old. A bunch of newspaper clippings appears. Ning Nong turns out to be the elephant that carried two British girls to safety when the tsunami crashed onto the beaches of Phuket. The girls were just taking a ride when Ning Nong felt the tremors and ran into the mountains, long before any human realised anything was wrong. The story hit the news worldwide, Ning Nong became famous instantly. But she's still here on her slab of concrete. And the family still lives in a hut, hidden away in the middle of this fancy place.

The families rack their brains in an effort to come up with information about Nung Ning. They call other mahouts. One of them mentions Phang Nga, a town north of Phuket. A truck carrying three elephants from Surin arrived there a year and a half ago. Phang Nga? That name has never been mentioned in this story, what about Phang Nga? I get a crash course in elephant trading. The mahouts teach, Lee translates, I listen.

Registering an elephant through legal channels in Phuket costs at least 640 euros for bribes. Therefore, many new owners take their elephant off the truck in Phang Nga, and walk into Phuket at night. So that's why only half of the elephants in Phuket are registered! Sometimes elephants meant for Phuket end up going to a different destination. To Krabi, for example, where it's easier to register elephants, and where an owner can earn big money in illegal logging. Elephants are wanted in Krabi, but on the other hand they can only leave if plenty of bribes are paid. The mahouts exchange info about tricks to get commissions. If you're smart enough, money can be made at the seller's as well as at the buyer's end.

Ning Nong needs bathing. A mahout, with his seven-month-old son on his beautifully tattooed arm, fills a bucket with soap suds. Ning Nong sits down on command, with her feet up to have her belly washed; then she turns on one side, and then on the other.

The boy sits in the bucket nearby. Still too small to walk, he pulls himself up on Ning Nong's ear and stands up straight. A budding mahout. 'That's how I grew up too,' Wichian says.

FantaSea's manager has by now checked out everything, but there's no Nung Ning at his theme park. He also mentions Phang Nga. On the beach that evening, we consider our options. Since we have no more business left in Phuket, we decide to take the bus to Phang Nga in the morning. *Nga* means tusk, as I remember from the *Chang* song. I ask Wichian what *phang* means. He puts his hands around an imaginary tusk and makes an explosive motion. Exploding tusk? I find out later, in fact, the name is a corruption of Phu Nga—Mount Nga.

On visiting an animal registration office for the umpteenth time, we find the Phang Nga civil servant helpful. First he goes through the folder of paperwork; no Nung Ning. Then the computer; still no Nung Ning. When he looks for the name of the man to whom Wichian has sold the prodigal daughter, he finds it, and, what's more, several elephants, including two that have arrived

Fig 14. Dok-ngeon and Antoinette, Surin (photo: Hanna Jongepier)

Fig 15. A pin behind Dok-ngeon's ear prevents her from turning her head

Fig 16. Negotiations with Wichian (on the left), Si-nuan's mahout

Fig 17. Trekking elephant in Phuket

Fig 18. Begging elephant near Doi Suthep temple, Chiang Mai (photo: Antoinette van de Water)

Fig 19. Beautiful Gold and Willowy Tree mate, Surin (photo: Hanna Jongepier)

Fig 20. Christmas camp in Surin (photo: Hanna Jongepier)

Fig 21. Dok-ngeon in the early morning, seen from the tent, Ayutthaya

Fig 22. Mahouts Duang, Wiset, and Narong

Fig 23. Radio FM 93.75 Mhz

Fig 24. Ayutthaya

Fig 25. Wiset, Dok-ngeon, Duang, and a budding mahout

Fig 26. The drawing contest

Fig 27. Prize winning drawing: 'We're going to bring you back to nature'

Fig 28. Elephant quiz in a primary school, Ayutthaya

from Surin a year and a half ago: Sao Noi and Som Wang. 'Those are the ones who were in the truck with Nung Ning!' Wichian says. How is this possible? Why have these two been registered and not Nung Ning?

We speed off to Island Safari, the camp where Sao Noi and Som Wang work. Lee and I drop in at the souvenir shop and keep the manager occupied, while Wichian goes on to the mahout accommodations. After a while, Wichian calls for Lee. Later, Lee phones that I have to come over, too. I can tell from the tone of his voice that he's got news. Nung Ning is here, she has to be! But it is bad news. Nung Ning is dead.

The mahouts say there were problems with Nung Ning. She didn't accept her mahout and attacked the owner. She needed extra training to be able to perform in shows. At night, on a short chain with the other young elephants, she behaved defiantly. That's why she was put outside, on a long chain, allowing her to eat. Three weeks after her arrival, she pulled a cable from a tree, put it in her mouth, and was electrocuted. She probably thought the cable was the garden hose she used to drink from. She was buried immediately. The park wanted to keep her death a secret. That's why the grave is hidden. There wasn't a farewell ceremony, and her death went unreported. An unregistered elephant doesn't exist, isn't taxable, and it doesn't die, either. So much easier.

Poor Nung Ning, whom I would have loved to reunite with her mother.

A *tuktuk* takes us to the airport. We book passage for Bangkok and leave rain-drenched Phuket. Now we must focus on the purchase of Dok-ngeon and Si-nuan, on planning the trip by truck, and on finishing the hassle with the permits.

5

Familiar Things

On the train from Bangkok to Chiang Mai, Lee and I discuss our plans for the months ahead. After buying Si-nuan and Dok-ngeon, I first want to take them camping in Surin to let them get used to each other and to their mahouts. Then we'll hit the road. A trip of about three weeks, with stops at three Thai cities. Preferably old cities, with lots of temples and elephant history. In each one we will pitch our tents for a week, try to get in touch with as many people from the local population as we can, and generate as much publicity as possible. Elephant classes for students, elephant rituals, conversations with officials, temple rituals, handing out posters, leaflets, and T-shirts. Basically, everything we had already planned for the walk.

As our first stopping place we choose Ayutthaya, the ancient capital of Siam. Thirty-three kings in a row held sway over the land there. At one time there had been a trading post of the Dutch East India Company in operation there. The name means 'unconquerable'. Ha, we'll see about that!

Then off to Lopburi, the city of temple ruins and macaques. I wonder if our sacred elephants can get along with these sacred monkeys. Finally, Sukhothai, which means 'dawn of happiness'. Again, an ancient city of kings; the ruins of palaces and temples have made it onto the Unesco World Heritage list. All three cities have a history in which elephants play a big part.

Lee seems a bit worried. 'We need permits to stay at these places with our elephants, and permits for transportation. We need to be well connected with the vets at the animal offices. And you have to watch out when people say 'no problem'. You turn around and suddenly: big problem!' He reads us a report from the newspaper. As from January 2006, the rules for the transportation of animals are very strict, due to avian flu. Some Chinese birds have already dropped dead from the sky onto Thai territory.

Travelling from south to north, we see the rice in the paddy fields at all stages of its growth, from little green transplanted sprouts in the water to the stubble in recently harvested fields. Sometimes the central part of Thailand looks a little like the Dutch countryside, flat and agricultural. Only here you see white egrets instead of black crows, golden Buddhas instead of church steeples, lotus flowers instead of duckweed. Outside the train, whole families are stooped over, ankle deep in mud in the flooded fields while transplanting the rice. Meanwhile, inside our railway carriage, our phones are bleeping. Among those, Lee's. A mahout from Phuket is calling about Nung Ning; he says he knows where she is. 'Never mind,' Lee says.

After twelve hours, we enter the mountains of northern Thailand where the forest begins. The tropical environment is so much more exuberant than ours. We have little beans, here there are trees with beans three feet long. Bamboo reaches for the heavens. Elephant country. Here we could have walked safely.

In the morning, we report at Lek's travel agency. The pick-up truck from the Elephant Nature Park is already purring happily outside. Quickly, I dump my dirty clothes, and stuff some clean ones into my bag; the travel agency functions as my baggage depot when I'm on the road. I also succeed in getting the manager of an elephant manure paper project on the phone, and arrange a visit in a couple of days. All phone calls have to be made now, because we won't have any connection up at the Park.

We're ready to leave now, and our first call is at the market to stock up on treats for the elephants. Bananas, cucumbers, melons, pumpkins; with two thousand pounds of snacks in the back, Pom and I drive off into the mountains. We squabble. Every time on my return after I have been away for a longer period of time, at first she ignores me for a while. I say I resent that, she says I'm too sensitive. Then she plays a tape of Palaporn & Punch, my favourite Thai musicians. We laugh, we're fine again. When we sight the Mae Taeng River winding its way through the valley below us, we also pass the first tourists from the trekking camps. They are in canopied carts, pulled by water buffaloes. Eventually we drive through the bamboo gate of the Park. The elephants have been waiting for us, they know what's in the back of our truck, and if the mahouts didn't prevent them, they would climb up on the back to get to it.

The central hut is full of tourists and volunteers. I'd been told that the number of day trippers had grown since Lek's appearance on television as Hero of Asia, but I wasn't prepared for this crowd! Everyone descends on the food, the volunteers to wash and serve everything up, the elephants to eat it.

No chains, no hooked goads, no wounds, good food. What a relief. No more contradictions for now.

Although . . . I used to work here as a volunteer, shovelling dung, cutting grass for the elephants in the morning, and digging mud holes. Now I'm being followed around by a camera crew and continually answering questions. After ten minutes of this, I feel like saying 'I don't know' to every question. The elephants are supposed to be the centre of attention, not somebody who has collected some money. I feel rather uncomfortable. Especially when the elephants go for a bath in the river and the volunteers, who always go along to scrub them down, have to stay behind for the camera crew to get a good shot of Lek, myself, and the elephants. Fortunately, things soon get back to normal after that. When the big dusty bodies lower themselves into the water, you can almost hear them cooling down. Their greyish brown hide turns a shiny black; sensually they recline on their sides and even slide underwater, leaving just their trunks held in the air to breathe through. Elephants are perfect snorkellers. They are such good swimmers they have been known to swim across estuaries. Because their bodies have large internal cavities, they can float almost like balloons. During wars, they were sometimes lined up as breakwaters in wild rivers to allow the army to cross safely behind them. Here the water flows fast as well, but not so swiftly that people will be swept away. Mahouts, volunteers, and brave day-trippers jump into the water with scoops and brushes to scrub down the animals. Elephants like to bathe twice a day, not just to cool down and for fun but also to rid themselves of insects and keep away infections. They can smell water from fifteen miles away, and in dry times they dig with their tusks and trunks in places where they sense water underground.

Jungle Boy, also known as the baby monster, causes alarm by swimming over to the other bank. In a few months, when we have raised enough funds for the purchase of that land, he can wander around over there as much as he likes. But for now it's off limits, as there are plantations where a five-year-old elephant can wreak havoc. His mahout Luang sprints after him and reaches him just in time; he climbs on his back and steers him back into the water. Jungle Boy is the best swimmer in the Park. When he was still at a trekking camp, he had to cross a river every day. He is a real imp. The only time I can actually get close to him is while he is bathing. When I climb on his back, he tries to grab my foot with his trunk and fling me off. But when I let myself float away, he quickly comes after me. I have to watch out for his little sharp tusks, and be careful not to end up between his floundering legs. Playing with the young elephants in the water is my favourite activity at the Park. Especially at this time, because it's the only place I can be on my own for a little while.

Mahouts and volunteers are mixed up in a waterfight by now and chase each other until everyone is out of breath and crawls back up onto the bank. The elephants blow dust and sand on themselves with their trunks, which helps to keep insects away as well.

The two bosom friends Jokia and Mae Perm are in the field next to the big hut. Jokia was blinded when an angry owner poked a sharp stick in her eyes. Even though elephants have naturally poor eyesight and perceive more with their trunk, blindness is still a serious handicap. Jokia has become fearful, she panics easily. Mae Perm accompanies her full time. You can always see the two ladies side by side, often with their trunks in each others mouths. A few years ago, they adopted Hope, by now a six-year-old male teenager. He challenges all the bulls at the Park. Every now and then they put him in his place and noisily drive him back dozens of feet. Mae Perm keeps an eye on Hope. Right now he is sparring with Jungle Boy. Mae Perm runs after them to protect him. Then Jokia panics and starts trumpeting loudly. Mae Perm stops and looks at Jokia, at Hope, then runs back to Jokia to pat her soothingly with her trunk. Meanwhile, both teenagers are being pulled apart by Lek and some mahouts. Hope is getting better at fighting his own battles. He is a *phlai si do*, a male without tusks. They are usually more aggressive than males with tusks, as if they have to compensate.

In the field, Lek does an interview with 'my' film crew, while playing with Kanoon. 'When you give an elephant love, he will give back love,' Lek says. It is the beginning and the end of her elephant teaching. 'Violence isn't needed. The goad is superfluous, chains around the leg are needed only in rare cases. When a bull is in musth, for example.' Musth is the rutting season, during which male elephants get unmanageable. According to Lek, many owners put bulls in musth on chains that are too short, and let them go hungry to weaken them physically. They do have to be chained up, she says, but it's best to do that in a shady place with enough drinking water and easily digestible food. 'Most elephant aggression is a response to the violence they have been treated with. To make them obey you, you have to reward them when they do things right, just like children. You can also use tricks. For instance, if we want them to walk faster, we throw dirt on their feet because they hate filth.' Lek is the best elephant whisperer I know.

I remember my first time at the Park, when we were having trouble keeping the babies Hope and Gingmai out of our huts. We would put everything out of trunk's reach, but they would still try and see how much they could get away with. Chasing them off didn't work, that was just more fun. Finally, we realised they were afraid of puppies. After that, whenever we saw a probing trunk appear, we would pick up a pup, and the elephant was gone.

'Elephants are quick to learn,' Lek teaches the film crew imperturbably. 'From people and from each other. They can live in harmony with us, often they are a part of the family. Our problem is that we don't have enough jungle for them.' She explains that under Thai law, domesticated or house elephants are considered private property, like cattle and fowl. That's why they are not protected like their cousins in the wild. 'The owner can do as he pleases. The government should pass a strong law that also protects the house elephant. Besides that, there should be environmental measures to stop deforestation.'

The interviewer wants to know why people are not allowed to ride the elephants at the Elephant Nature Park. 'Of course they can easily carry a human. But they have had plenty of tourists on their back in the past, let them walk around or stand still as they please.' In trekking camps, things often go awry when the animals get wounds because of the howdahs. They are kept working without the open sores being attended to, because time is money. The wooden pins that Dok-ngeon had had behind her ears are often used in trekking camps as well. Tourists don't notice any of this. There is also the baby issue. In the wild, a baby won't move even six feet away from his mother, never. A youngster is being fed, protected, and raised non-stop. When the mother has to carry tourists around, the baby suffers. It is for good reasons that in trekking camps the sexual instincts often disappears, just as in zoos. 'We have to educate tourists,' says Lek, 'they have to help us abolish these practices.'

Dinner is good that evening, as always. The wives of the mahouts cook. There's enough to choose from, so that if you want you can have a completely vegetarian meal. The mahouts like to tease the volunteers from time to time. 'Mmmm, dog barbecue tonight!' Large crickets fly around my head, a beetle settles in my food, a moth slides down inside the neck of my shirt. The elephants are grazing peacefully. Soon Si-nuan and Dok-ngeon will be among them, no one can stop it now. Plan B is taking shape. We turn in early. Tomorrow morning we'll take the film crew and a group of elephants to Elephant Haven, the forest area across the river where the animals can roam free.

***

Boonkhum is an approximately fifty-year-old bull. Lek took him to Elephant Haven in 2001. He had lost all faith in humans. In his life he had already seen every nook and cranny of the labour market: logging, shows, begging. An elephant jack-of-all-trades and finally master of none anymore—someone stripped him of his ivory tusks.

Two pounds of ivory will fetch 50,000 baht on the open market. It is possible to partially saw off a tusk without physically hurting the elephant. Tusks are extremely long incisors, which consist of hollow shafts containing a nerve that takes up about one third of the tusk length. When sawing, one has to be very careful not to touch the nerve. With Boonkhum, that is what happened nevertheless. He must have been in agony since finally one tusk fell out. The hole became infected, and the infection first spread across his face and then across his body. When he was found on a Jumbo Express trip, he seemed to have given up on life. His wounds were cleaned, he was given medication. After he had recuperated, he was moved to the Park. Since then his other tusk has regrown—tusks grow about three inches a year, throughout an elephant's life—but the hole left by the lost tooth still has to be cleaned and treated daily. The infection hasn't gone away; when he is in musth and the festering wound cannot be cleaned, puss leaks out of his eyes.

Today Boonkhum walks at the rear of the caravan, grazing and sniffing. You wouldn't think it when you see them go at it, but in the wild elephants do a good deal of conservation. With everything they gulp down, they also swallow seeds. When they discharge them, undigested, fifteen miles down the road, the seeds can germinate on the spot, fertilised by the manure supplied with them. *Et voilà*, another tree has been planted. An elephant that has enough space to roam will never graze an area to the ground. Like a prudent housewife, he will always leave enough behind to provide plenty to eat upon a return visit.

We walk calmly on. An elephant goes at about the same pace as a human. Apart from the occasional sound of breaking branches, our caravan makes hardly a sound. Here the elephants are in charge. I feel proud we are able to show this to the film crew. When we arrive in Elephant Haven, everybody is satisfied with the progress on the film so far. Beer soon adds another wellspring of content. By the time the charcoal fire for our meal is blazing, the elephants have disappeared; only Boonkhum sticks around. He'll stay close to us all through the night. Before we get down to dinner, Pom goes off into the forest with Bud, Boonkhum's mahout, to find medicinal plants for the treatment of the gaping cavity in his jaw. Bud climbs the tall, slick tree trunks like a woodpecker to collect leaves and branches. Pom provides a commentary: 'Mai du, good for closing open wounds. Mai soh, when you're itching from dirty water. Tiger Smell, to stop the bleeding. The medication works for humans and elephants,' she says.

By the time we finish dinner, it's almost dark. We drive off the chill of the evening at this altitude with a fire. Bochu, Lilly's mahout, plays a frisky tune on his bamboo flute. I start to read a book about Aung San Suu Kyi, the woman who is a figurehead of the struggle against the generals in Burma. I notice the mahouts are talking about it. When I pass them the book; they leaf through it from front to back, looking for names they know. They recognise people in the photographs of students' marches. They ask me to translate passages.

Narong gives me something to eat, a nut with some white paste wrapped in a leaf. Yuck! Revolting! It takes at least half a bottle of beer for the taste to disappear. 'Betel nut,' Pom says. 'People chew it because it drives away fatigue.' The mahouts do magic tricks and although I don't get them at all, it is great fun. 'Oh my Buddha,' Narong calls out, imitating the American tourists who call out 'Oh my God!' every time they come face to face with an elephant. 'Come on, guys, to bed,' Pom says. 'Tomorrow you can play again.'

I get under my blanket, close to the fire. From far away comes the sound of the wooden bells the elephants wear around their necks. Four years ago I could hear chainsaws, but not anymore. Boonkhum's huge skull scrapes along the platform we lie on. I hear his breathing, hollow because of the hole. It sounds like that villain from Star Wars, what's his name again . . . the betel nut doesn't do anything for me . . . I sleep.

In the morning, the sun lights up the edge of the mountainside across from us. Somewhere below a deep, long moaning is heard, like an elephant stretching. Then a bang. 'Hunters,' Pom says. A fire is already burning, while on it is a huge cauldron with the evil looking medication for Boonkhum. During breakfast, Pom recounts how she once tried in vain to attend an elephant training course. Nowadays young elephants have to be trained at the so-called Elephant Conservation Centre, an official government organisation where mahouts are trained as well. Can girls be mahouts? 'Sure,' Pom says. 'But some women might be too tender-hearted. You have to be gentle, but brave as well. You must have the courage to feed a bull, even when he is in musth.' It would be a great way to find out what is really going on. Maybe I should apply for mahout school.

The elephants are nowhere to be seen, and we don't hear the bells, either. But the mahouts paid attention during the night, they have an idea of where to look. They're heroes, these guys. They don't just take care of the elephants, they can also cook, track, clean, play the flute, play doctor, and do magic. During a fire a year ago, they stormed right through the bushes up the slope and put out the fire with branches and cloths.

We look for the prodigal sons and daughters for about four hours, on trails so steep it's hard to imagine an elephant using them. Especially downhill. Because of the enormous weight of the head, tusks, neck, and trunk, elephants must be careful not to have their front legs give way; they have been known to descend shuffling on their bum. We find our elephants just below a mountain top, grazing in the shade of the trees. Wiset, a young mahout, uses his elephant's leg to climb onto her neck. '*Sung, sung*! Lift your leg,' he says to Mae Boon Ma. He grabs her ear, steps on her foot, then on the upper leg that is held horizontally, and pulls himself up. It is wonderful to see how perfectly an elephant responds to its mahout. Narong loves to make his elephant trumpet when there are many people nearby. Almost unseen he gives a signal, the trunk goes up in the air and blares like crazy. People take off in a flurry, and Narong watches with an innocent smile.

On the road back, Bochu saves my life. Suddenly a bee is buzzing around my head, then another one, and another one . . . Killer bees! A whole swarm of killer bees! I know I shouldn't strike at them, but do it anyway. Just before I am completely seized by panic, Bochu appears and swipes the bees back into the forest with a few huge whacks from his scarf. Relieved I thank him, but he just laughs a bit. Oh well, may be not killer bees, I really couldn't see them all that well.

Before we move on to the Park, Boonkhum's suppurating cavity is treated. Pom rinses it out with water that is led to the hut through a hose, from a nearby mountain stream. Her arm disappears inside up to her armpit. After that, Bud fills a kind of bicycle pump with liquid medicine and squirts it into the hole. Boonkhum takes a step back, but on the whole he is cooperative.

The walk back is faster than the one up. The animals know there's a cool river waiting for them downhill. We cross it on the bamboo raft. We are tired, it was wonderful. Back to civilisation.

***

Upon arrival back in the city, I immediately go looking for a computer and put out my feelers on the Internet. It has been days since I opened my e-mail.

More people who want to join the walk. A Canadian man wants to donate money to buy the temple elephant of Doi Suthep. First the man from St. Petersburg, now this guy! Perhaps we should establish a fund so people can donate money to buy street elephants. On the other hand, the available land is limited as well. We need more Elephant Nature Parks.

The organisation of *Bring the elephant home* in the Netherlands also needs attention. Sometimes it's hard to manage from Thailand. They're all volunteers, and of course, things go wrong from time to time. Still, I like to lead a small organisation like this. You can keep track of every aspect, you know every nook and cranny. To start something from nothing and make it grow, that's my kind of thing.

The Elephant Dung Paper Project sounds better in English than in Dutch, but it still is what it says. On our way back to Bangkok, where the film crew will get on a plane home and I will pick up Hanna, we visit Lampang, 150 miles south of Chiang Mai, to take a look at the project. It might be a good way to keep elephants without hurting them.

The project is housed in the Elephant Conservation Centre, the government organisation that combines training with a show and a hospital. The centre turns out to be a large, park-like landscape. Signs point out the way to the restaurant, the souvenir shop, the show, and the Royal Stables. So even royal elephants are housed here. Wanchai Asawawibulkij, the paper project manager, is waiting for us. He might just be the only person in the world whose business card shows a beautiful turd. Of course the card is made of elephant dung paper, very pretty. Paper can be made of dung because it contains many crushed fibres, still visible in the card. And no, it doesn't smell.

Wanchai takes us through the process, from loading the dung at the stables, through washing and cooking, to draining it through screens, and finally letting these dry out in the sun. Real handmade paper; and it requires nothing more to produce than dung, water, fire, a little hydrogen peroxide, and some optional colouring agents. And manpower of course. The waste water is used to extract bio gas, which the mahout families use for cooking. Five people work at the factory, plus about ten more in support. They use the paper to make all sorts of things for sale at the shop. 'We have fifty elephants in all,' Wanchai tells us. 'We use about four hundred pounds of dung a day, that's what ten elephants produce. With this we make two hundred and fifty sheets. We would like to make more, but there's no market for that yet. Marketing and export are priorities.'

According to Wanchai, the elephants here lead a good life. In the evening, they go into the forest, and they don't have to play soccer in the shows. 'It's all natural, they only show how they used to pull logs in the logging industry,' he says innocently. The Elephant Conservation Centre is known for its elephant orchestra, and the artistic qualities of the elephant paintings are highly praised. But Wanchai means well. 'I hope the project will help in getting elephants off the streets. The government should gather them together, like they are here, where people can come and see them, and where the dung can be used to make paper. I believe many Thai people want to protect the elephants.'

***

It is hot and stuffy in Bangkok. Thanon Prachasongkhrao, a street near my guesthouse, is a pressure cooker. At ground level, every building has a shop, while the pavement in front of them is largely occupied by market booths, especially where the night market springs up after sundown. Hot food, cold food, raw food, red, blue, and yellow food. Stalls for cell phones, gold jewellery, plastic combs. A one-person sewing workshop, a cobbler, an insect booth, a lady pulling squid through a press. Through it all, traffic roars day and night, as it does everywhere in Bangkok.

An elephant-headed figure stands on the corner of Prachasongkhrao Road. It's made of gold with four human arms and a human body. His name is Phra Phikhanet, it is the Thai version of the Hindu god Ganesh. Buddhism and Hinduism are good neighbours. All day long, people come to kneel in front of his shrine, offering floral wreaths and burning incense. 'He bring luck, very lucky,' according to Mrs. Kawruen, who comes here every day to pray. Her marriage was saved, her son is back on the straight and narrow path, all because of Phra Phikhanet. But there are live elephants here as well, she says. '*Mai di!*' Not good!

Come sunset at the night market, I spot one among the two-, three-, and four-wheeled vehicles on the road. When the market closes, she will get some of the fruit that hasn't been sold. Her name is Um-bun, the mahout says. She is three years old and comes from Surin. Where will she sleep tonight?

That same night I see another street elephant on Sukhumvit, one of Bangkok's large shopping arteries. The side streets are lined with hotels and bars, the pavements bulge with booths offering imitation brand products and Thai silk. There Fong Peng appears, a three-year-old female elephant, from Surin as well. She is accompanied by a young couple and an elderly man. They look like homeless strays, all four of them.

At the end of their shoot, the film crew would like to find a camp where the mahout beggars and their elephants hide out during the day. Finding such a location proves to be difficult. Fortunately, the son of an acquaintance of a relative of the driver of the mini-van knows of a place. To find it, though, seems like an endless search as we drive along city motorways, sometimes at ground level, then up on the superhighway elevated on pillars. Office blocks and slums pass by, seamlessly interlaced. In the end, a police officer shows us the place. There, close to Rama IX Road, where the new part of the express highway is being built, you see? Close to a spaghetti junction of fly-overs, we see a wasteland littered with junk interspersed with wispy trees, grass, and brushwood. Near the entrance lie broken spirit houses, car tires, plastic bags. The traffic roars in the background, a plane soars overhead every now and then. In among the brushwood, tarpaulins are rigged, providing shelter for the mats and the other necessities of the mahouts that stay here during the day. It's a group of three men and three women. They are putting sugarcane and cucumber in plastic bags as food for the elephants to sell to tourists that night. A bit further on, next to a pool of stagnant water, stand two trucks for transporting the elephants from and to Surin.

The eldest of the mahouts, a good-looking, friendly man, about fifty years old, with beautiful tattoos on his arms and chest, is willing to speak with us. His name is Ok Salangam. The elephants are two, nine, and ten years old, he tells us. They're already trained, they can handle traffic and people. Every night the mahouts walk them to Sukhumvit, the tourist shopping street. Several hours to get there, several hours back. On a good day they make eighty euros, on a bad day thirty. That seems a lot, compared to the three euros a day that mahouts at the Elephant Nature Park get. But it has to be shared out among six people, as well as with the family back home. And the costs are high, like the lease of the trucks.

The group has been in Bangkok for a week, and they'll probably go back to Surin in another week. They have to keep an eye out for the police all the time. 'The regular police are no problem, they usually leave us alone. Another government department is more dangerous; they are after us because we are not allowed to camp here. When they find us, we go to prison first. Then we have to go to Chonburi, where our documents are checked. If they are in order, we will be releasedlitt without being fined. But we lose a lot of money because of the travelling and not being able to work.'

Sometimes they visit Bangkok several times a year, sometimes only once. 'It is not a good job, I would rather stay at home. But there's no work for elephants in Surin, at the most a wedding or a burial ritual. We can't do without the income from begging, and here the elephants get better food than back home. Just look around, so much grass and it doesn't belong to anyone! In Surin free elephant food doesn't exist anymore. Every bit of land has an owner.'

Ok Salangam is one of the Suai, the tribe that has lived with elephants for centuries. Today he owns only one. 'First I had the mother, but she died after she had a baby. That baby is part of your family, you care for it. I'm a truck driver, but elephants are my passion.' His younger brother trains the elephants. 'Training begins when they are two years old. They learn all the tricks: standing on their hind legs, bowing, the usual stuff. When you train them young, you don't need to use violence. It's the same as with people, some people hit their children, others don't. You can go far by rewarding them. But the older they are, the more difficult it gets.'

6

Rescues

IN DECEMBER THE northeast of Thailand starts to dry up. The skies are a very clear blue, the fields a pale yellow, the irrigation canals have no water in them. While Dok-ngeon and Si-nuan are waiting in Surin for their rescue, further up north, the first permit is finally issued. Mae Taeng, the district where the Park is situated, gives us a document with lots of stamps and signatures, which says that the elephants are welcome. With this, we can start on the rest of the red tape.

In early December, Lee, Hanna, Yut, Nong, and I explore the route we'll take with the elephants from Surin. We'll look for temples where we can camp, and for schools we can visit. Over time, my vision of our camp sites has become romantic. I imagine small, quiet temples, serenely peaceful, meditating monks, green oases along flowing creeks. Cooking in front of the tent, while the elephants paddle. It isn't long before I have to throw my rose-tinted glasses out of the window. It's not easy to find places where our team as well as the elephants can stay. Either the area is not green enough, or there's no shade, no camp site, no water. At some places, the temple management can't be found, or there are monkeys in cages, or the temple hill is simply too steep for the elephants. So in the end we're quite happy to find a modern concrete temple near a canal in Ayutthaya, a beautiful temple near a noisy motorway in Lopburi, and a temple with a little teak grove in Sukhothai.

With several school headmasters, we discuss our ideas about an elephant day for their students. During one such talk, while Lee is taking care of details, I sit on a little doorstep trying to cool down, a pack of street dogs surrounding me. The animals are mangy, have filthy wounds, and are covered with fleas. Hey, I think, since we'll have a vet along with us for the elephants anyway . . . we could bring medications and set up a free mobile animal clinic everywhere we go. In this way we can help these animals, and at the same time generate publicity. Good idea, Lee agrees.

After the successful scouting expedition, we drive back to Surin on a mile-stone trip: to buy Dok-ngeon and Si-nuan. But at Lek's request, we first visit the Madee family, owners of the elephant with the crippled hind leg that she had bought at the festival, and who is still with her owners. We are going to finalise the documentation and make arrangements for transportation to the Park.

Duang Madee, the almost sixty-year-old head of the family, is an old hand in the mahout trade. As far back as he knows, his ancestors have been mahouts. After the sale of Malai Thong to Lek, his family has only one elephant left. These days Duang is out in the fields all day long, for he is afraid they will catch fire because of the drought. Twenty elephants from his village have already left for the city.

Duang bought Malai Thong, 'Golden Garland,' three years ago in a province near the Burmese border. She was working in the logging industry when she stepped on a landmine. The family believed they could heal the foot, but she has never been able to work again. The other elephant, Mae Thongbai or 'Golden Leaf', has been with the family for twenty years, so she is a family member. Duang's son and daughter-in-law will take her to the city next week, because there is no more food in Surin. I like the Madee family. They treat their animals well. They are poor and have to choose between two evils: go to the city or sell the elephant. While we're at Duang's home, the neighbours casually offer us their baby elephant.

***

When we stopped to see Dok-ngeon in her field last time, I didn't bring her any food. I won't make that mistake again. We buy up half the market and drive the mini-van, loaded with bananas, cucumbers, and pineapples, to the owner's village. He leads the way to the field, flanked by two mahouts with sunglasses and gold necklaces. We find Dok-ngeon on land that's been clear cut, with some eucalyptus trees and dried up grass around the edges. Beneath the mud on her skin I can see blood. She is very hungry. With one bunch of bananas still in her mouth, she already reaches for the next one in my hands. She empties two large bags of bananas and a bag of cucumbers in one go. She just squeezes the pineapple juice into her mouth, the rest ends up on the ground. When I try to negotiate with the owner, the two mahouts begin to shout. The owner doesn't seem willing to lower his price. We make a new offer of 7,700 euros, 1,300 more than last time, but still 1,300 below his November asking price. We give him time to think about it; with these mahouts around, there's no point in negotiating anyway. Before we go, the owner chains Dok-ngeon's front legs together and shackles her to a tree. So she won't graze the field clear too quickly, he explains.

I don't trust these people, I would prefer to take Dok-ngeon away from here today. Pending the permits, we need a place to leave the elephants with an easy mind. 'Lee, how about the Madee family? What if we pay them to take care of them for three weeks?' Lee picks up his phone, it is arranged in the blink of an eye. One worry less. The next day Dok-ngeon's owner calls: 7,700 euros. Seven hundred more than the asking price at the festival. But I don't care anymore, Dok-ngeon has to be rescued from this misery. And because we have called off the walk, there is some money left in our budget.

It's immensely crowded at the bank, the computer has crashed, and I can't withdraw any money with my personal credit card. For three hours, we try every possible way to worm some money out of the bank, in vain. The bank clerk tells me I have to open an account, as the amount is too large to be paid out at once. That takes another hour. Then the money has to be transferred. I'm sorry, Dok-ngeon, another day gone, just hang on.

With the sale of Si-nuan in mind, I call the Postbank in Holland to raise the limits of my personal credit card—with my business credit card, I can only get money from a cash point, which limits the cashable amount. They promise to take care of it within sixteen hours. The next day I hopefully put my card in the machine. Nothing. At home, the Postbank has a blue, Disney-like lion mascot visible at every festival, every advertising opportunity; but if you need them to buy elephants, forget it. We're almost about to rob the bank, when two Dutch people behind us offer to try their cards. Fortunately, they have them in all sorts and colours. To our unspeakable relief and gratitude, they manage to gather the money with seven separate withdrawals.

Before I turn in that night, I get out the heaps of money, counting it over again and again and making neat piles of ten thousands. All of it from support-ers, from the benefit festival, from the Theresia School, through the website, from the Friends of the Elephant festival. There it is, on my hotel bed, and we're going to use it to buy street elephants. I imagine disaster scenarios. The documents are fake, the documents don't belong to the right elephants, they are gone after the transaction, owners have changed their minds, I lose the money. Stay calm. No one can stop me now.

In the morning, Lee has already started on the paperwork for Dok-ngeon. We have to get postal stamps to send a copy of the contract to the animal district office in Chiang Mai immediately. At the city office, we get registration stamps for the documents; in the event something goes wrong, at least the documents are legally valid. Next, back to the animal district office we visited two weeks ago. Because of a festival, there is a cheerful atmosphere, happy police officers are grouped around a bottle of Mekong whiskey. Dok-ngeon's owner is waiting for us, in good spirits. Countless stamps, signatures, and bank notes later, and Dok-ngeon is finally free.

We arrive at her field with an empty truck. She comes hopping over to us with her front legs tied together. The chains come off, and Lee and I climb into the luggage compartment at the back of the cabin to make her feel at ease during the trip. It's not even necessary, she seems to like it just fine. Lee and I are elated. We sing songs for Dok-ngeon and sniff the wind. It smells like freedom. When I look at the little elephant, my hair blowing in the wind and the setting sun on my skin, I am beside myself with happiness.

The Madee family has laid on a feast for Dok-ngeon, there is a mountain of banana trees, palm leaves, and bananas. All the villagers come to take a look at this *farang*, this stranger with her elephant. They stand next to me to see how tall I am, pinch my arms, compare the colour of our skins, and keep pointing at their noses laughingly. Duang's daughter-in-law says Dok-ngeon is lucky, she has been saved from a bad owner. Duang washes her wrinkly head to treat the wounds. She has been beaten up. On the left part of her forehead is a hole with a yellow liquid oozing out. Duang puts my hand on the head to feel the mushiness under the skin; it's all puss underneath. He cleans the open wounds and disinfects them. Then we leave her in peace.

***

Ban Tha Klang is Si-nuan's village. It is also at the heart of the elephant tradition in the province of Surin. It has the largest elephant population density in Thailand. In the year 2000, researchers counted 124 elephants among 200 families, but the number has grown since then because the villagers keep buying elephants for begging.

Today we have more time to look around than last time. Most houses have a built-on, twelve-foot high stable. On the streets you find ivory cutters. This is the heart of Suai country. In past centuries, the Suai lived isolated from the outside world. Among them a special religion has developed, with Hindu gods, Buddhism, and elephants in it. When the Indians arrived with their religion in Southeast Asia about seventeen centuries ago, they brought along their knowledge of elephants. The Suai learned to discern 'good' elephants from 'bad' ones, gained knowledge about domesticating and riding them, and were initiated in magical elephant spells and elephant curses. Since then they have always cherished it. The Suai have helped kings catch and train wild elephants, and their animals were used in wars. In times of peace, they served their owners in forestry, carrying loads, and as household friends.

The inhabitants of the present-day Ban Tha Klang still possess this ancient knowledge and skill. The village lives with the animals, physically and spiritually. It has elephant statues, elephant traffic signs, elephant logos, elephant trucks, elephant dung, elephant footprints, and an elephant temple with an elephant graveyard. When an elephant dies, the family always has a farewell funeral ceremony. Some families bury the elephant for a year, then exhume the bones, and take them to the temple where they will be registered and preserved. Others bury their elephants at the temple and give them real headstones. Ultimately, they may cremate the bones, and keep the ashes in an urn.

There is another possibility, which is not widely spoken about. I learned about it from an elephant expert who had witnessed many burials. 'The farewell ceremonies are beautiful. Afterwards, people with sharpened knives are ready to take the meat off the bones and conserve it. They eat it. They are poor, an elephant is a huge supply of food. They will never slaughter it for its meat, they love it too much for that. When it dies, they cry just as much as when a brother dies.' But how about those elephant gods? And who would eat a dead family member? For a vegetarian like me, it is incomprehensible.

The most respected man in Ban Tha Klang is the eldest elephant shaman. Such a shaman is an expert in catching wild elephants, and knows all about secret curses, magic, and rituals. Becoming a shaman is the highest honour in life, and taking part in a hunting expedition means a man's life is well spent. I suppose it's something like the pilgrimmage to Mecca for Muslims. But while that still happens every year, the hunting expeditions of Ban Tha Klang have been over since the 1970s. All the same, before every important decision, advice is still asked from Phrakhru Prakram, a legendary mahout of days long gone, whose spirit resides in a statue revered in the village. He is the absolute star of the densely populated spirit world, which exists parallel to the everyday life of the villagers, and which seeps through every seam of Buddhism.

Ban Tha Klang is situated on the Moon River. And, a rare thing in Surin, it is in between two forests. That's why it is such a suitable environment for elephants. Or rather that's why it *used* to be a suitable environment; today the forests are privately owned and elephants are no longer allowed in. Nowadays food has to be bought at the market, for which the mahouts don't have the money. The city is their last option.

Si-nuan is not at home, Wichian has taken her to a neighbouring province to beg. We call him, and I have Lee offer him a new price, almost six thousand euros. If he agrees, he has to bring Si-nuan back. He can be back in two days, he says. We use the break in our trading activities to get acquainted with Ban Tha Klang. On route to an 'Elephant Study Centre' with our mini-van, we are in luck when we ask an elderly couple, Mr. Boonma (79), and his wife Saendee (78), for directions. They would like to ride along. Mr. Boonma is a shaman. He used to live in Mae Taeng in the north of Thailand, where the Elephant Nature Park is. In those days, he caught lots of wild elephants, first in Thailand, but when they became scarce, across the border in Cambodia and Laos as well. Ever since the Khmer Rouge killed the members of a hunting expedition in Cambodia, and the war in Vietnam spread across the entire region, the tradition has come to an end. Although knowledge and culture are still passed on, the actual hunt, as a communal venture shrouded in ceremony and taboo, is something of the past. There are no young shamans. Which doesn't mean wild elephants aren't caught anymore.

Mr. Boonma now works for the province of Surin, as the leader of a programme for elderly mahouts. He invites us to his home, where he puts on his traditional shaman clothes, woven from silk made in the village. He pulls out a horn, the horn of a water buffalo, from which he draws trumpet-like sounds. This is how shamans would send messages to each other on hunting expeditions, about the movements of the herd they were following, or about imminent danger. Mr. Boonma blows several tones in his living room, with a dreamy but also resolute look in his eyes, as he begins to reminisce. He tells us about the hunt. 'We would always go in a group, the eldest shaman was the leader. Sometimes we would be away for six months, on our tame elephants.

When we spotted a wild herd, we tried to surround it. Then it would get dangerous. When the wild elephants tried to run, our tame ones had to stop them. We picked out the young animals, they are easier to catch and to train.'

The capture was achieved with a rope, dozens of feet long, made of plaited strips of buffalo hide. The tail-end was tied in a loop that was positioned in front of the elephant's hind leg, using a long stick. If he stepped in the loop, it was pulled tight, and the battle between the wild and the tame elephant could commence. The rope was the hunters' single most important tool. It is animated by the spirit of Phrakhru Prakram, the legendary mahout.

Mr. Boonma takes us to a small shrine in the back of his garden, where his rope is laid on a small platform, surrounded by flowers and incense. Only he is allowed to touch it. There are many more taboos about the hunt. Maybe, I think, to ward off danger. When you stick to the rules, things will end well. For example, the expedition members would speak in code. Nobody was permitted to step over the rope. Dancing, singing, or fighting were not allowed. The expedition leader had to eat and drink before the others, and at night, while sleeping, everybody's head had to point in his direction.

There were several taboos on the home front as well. The shaman's house should not be swept when he was away on an expedition. Nobody was allowed to sit or lie on his bed. Only his family members could sleep in the house. The shaman's wife could not wear make-up, comb her hair, wear pretty clothes, sing, or dance. Female family members were not allowed to sit on a wooden bench with a man. If the prohibitions didn't manage to protect the hunter, then at least they would protect his marriage, I think disrespectfully.

***

Every mahout will tell you training is necessary. Without it, an elephant is unreliable among humans and can cause horrifying damage. In Ban Tha Klang, a welcoming ceremony precedes the training of a newly captured elephant. He is also given a name, or rather, he takes one, by choosing from four piles of food that represent four names.

First, the elephant has to get used to people. In the days of the hunt, he used to be tethered to a tame elephant during this stage, for about fifteen to thirty days. They would spend the day side by side. The tame elephant acted as teacher, confidant, and guard, all at the same time. When the wild elephant eventually calmed down and started to eat normally, he was locked into the wooden cage in which he would be taught to obey the mahout.

Since the hunt has been banned, and since cruelty in training has been exposed—by Lek among others—nobody openly talks about hunting or training. But obviously wild elephants are still coming in from Laos, Cambodia, and Burma, and just as evidently, there is still training and cruelty. Lek filmed it; an elephant researcher and a mahout from Surin told me about it; and I have seen for myself the wounds received by elephants in training. Pain is a means to break the will, at least in the beginning. With some animals only a little pain is needed, with others a lot. To discipline the elephant further, he gets the *tham* around his neck. It is a short, thick rope of buffalo hide with sharp points in between the leather. Or he gets sharpened pieces of wood behind his ears, as I found on Dok-ngeon. Above all, he learns to fear the hooked goad.

Mr. Boonma and his wife have welcomed us so graciously, and have told us about their lives with elephants with so much passion, that I am completely overwhelmed. Because I know more now, I have more respect. But it makes me feel the contradictions even more keenly. How many elephant families has Mr. Boonma torn apart? I know that many traditional mahouts feel nothing but love for their animals, but I also know the old classifications of mahouts. *Reghawan* are mahouts who control their elephants with love, *yukthiman* use cleverness, and *balwan* cruelty. Cruelty happens, of that I am absolutely certain. If not, what could be the source of the list of objectionable mahout behaviour that I found in an official mahout manual?

Never give an elephant addictive medicine, like amphetamines, opium, marihuana, or other kinds of drugs.

Don't pour or spray turpentine on the body of a sick elephant to get him to stand up, because the skin will get infected and peel off.

Never use heat (boiling water or fire) to get an elephant into a truck, or get him to work, because he can get hurt and die, or get mentally disturbed.

Never use a catapult, bow and arrow, rifles, handguns, gas rifles, .22-guns, airgun, or any other weapon to shoot at an elephant to scare him into doing what you want.

Everybody I ask, says the same thing: once an elephant is trained well, when the mahout is experienced and skilled, violence is no longer needed. All you have to do is show the goad and the animal will comply. According to the mahout manual:

> The goad is the single most important tool of the mahout. He should carry it whenever he is with the elephant, and he must be able to use it in such a way he doesn't wound the elephant. Novice mahouts must be told explicitly that the goad is not meant to inflict pain. He has to put pressure on precisely defined control points, which the elephant has learned to respond to.

The outstanding question is whether training really has to involve violence. Lek says it doesn't. Ok Salangam, the mahout leader in Bangkok, says it depends on the elephant, and on the mahout. In the mahout manual, I read that elephant training resembles the training of wild horses. That inspires hope. Nowadays, practically everybody is familiar with the horse whisperer, who tamed wild horses by studying their behaviour, and using that knowledge in a gentle way. Maybe there's a future for an elephant whisperer like Lek.

We say goodbye to Mr. Boonma and his wife and drive to the Elephant Study Centre, a government initiative sponsored by Thai Airways. When it was established, it was supposed to offer mahouts and elephants an alternative to migration. Elephants were supposed to do shows, tourists would provide income. We find a large open field, with two baby elephants and a female on a tight chain in the sun. We are mobbed by people selling fruit and ivory. With a few bunches of bananas, I walk over to the baby elephants who, according to the mahout, have just been separated from their mothers and are about to undergo training. They have wounds on all of their legs, the skin is peeling. I see abrasions around their necks as well. The younger one is called Phu Phan, after a mountain range in Surin. Her front legs are tied together and she is very hungry. Are these the only elephants in training? 'All the elephants in the area are trained here,' the mahout says, 'but it often takes place in other locations. Just come back at the end of the afternoon, most training happens at that time.'

I prepare for hell and damnation, but things turn out better than I expected. Two mahouts untie Phu Phan and guide her across the road. She has to get used to traffic and humans. Every day the mahouts take her for a walk, a little further every time. As a reward, she is patted on the head and sometimes gets a banana. The mahouts hold her ear and yell commands, every now and then they hang the hooked goad behind her ear. If we have some time left tomorrow morning, the mahout says, we can witness a mating.

***

Thongdee, 'Beautiful Gold', limps towards us with a chain on her foot. She was born with a bad leg and walks poorly. She is Phu Phan's mother; her owner wants her to give birth to more babies. For a mating, he pays the owner of the male 65 euros, 650 euros if a baby is born. Just like humans, elephants have children between the ages of fifteen and fifty, but in captivity procreation often fails to take place. It's as if they want to spare the offspring their own fate.

Here in Surin, too, elephants are increasingly a commodity. During the mid-1990s, 170 elephants were registered in the entire province, yet now there are 800. Many are bought to be resold for a profit. Over and over, I hear the same story, that the governor of the province is alleged to own 200 elephants himself. They supposedly work in the trekking camps of Chiang Mai, in shows in Bangkok, in Phuket, Pattaya, and on the streets. What's more, the number of families said to own one or two elephants are expanding as well. A father has his son earn money with their elephant on the streets or in a camp. And that yields enough money to buy another elephant.

Thongdee is tied between two trees, her hind legs spread. Then along comes Liew Yu, 'Willowy Tree', accompanied by a mahout who behaves as if he is sending a boxer into the ring. Willowy Tree is a large bull. The mahout orders him to approach and himself sits down underneath Beautiful Gold. Two other mahouts firmly hold her in place with their hooked goads held to her head. When she starts to protest loudly, the mahout underneath her picks up a knife and holds the tip to her stomach. He then grasps the huge penis of his elephant and tries to direct it. When Willowy Tree gives a good thrust, the penis shoots through his hands and hits him hard in the face. After about three attempts intercourse is achieved. Beautiful Gold is subsequently patted on the head while the bull is taken away. I have seen a mating at the Elephant Nature Park, as well. That wasn't gentle either, but at least the elephants themselves decided if they were ready, and the female was flanked by two girlfriends.

Later on, I naively write about the mating on the website under the heading 'forced sex', and score thousands of hits in the following week.

That night, Hanna and I get our Thai nicknames. Hardly any Thai is called by his long tongue-twisting formal name, they all have short nicknames, sometimes with teasing undertones. Lek (Little One), Ped (Duck), or Nok (Bird). It's about time we had them, too.

Hanna's name comes from the kitchen. Our not eating beef is one thing. Yut and the others know about that custom from Hindu people. But chicken and fish are not sacred animals, are they? And besides, they taste much better than the *taohu* (tofu or soyabean curd) Hanna likes so much. Taohu, that's a good name for Hanna.

After dinner Yut, Nong, Hanna, and I go for a night of Thai karaoke. For two euros an hour, you can rent your own karaoke room. A couch, a television with awe-inspiring speakers, a book with songs, a remote control, and room service. When you walk past the rooms, you hear people bellowing along with popular Thai hit songs. Singing like mad, throat wetted with a couple of Chang beers, there's no better way to blow off steam. I have no idea of what we're singing, but I know the songs from Chiang Mai night life, and the lines appear on screen in phonetics. Together with Hanna, I sing a song by the duo Palaporn & Punch. It ends with *tha dai song roi*, give me two hundred baht. Nong gets the giggles when Hanna sings this to me. '*Checkbin: song roi!*' she screams. '*Checkbin*' means bill, I use that word often because I have to keep accounts of all financial transactions. From now on, *checkbin* is not just collecting receipts, keeping the books, and paying salaries, but also my nickname. When we're at the market and Nong wants to buy something, she calls out: '*Checkbin, song roi!*' At the end of the afternoon, Yut *checkbins* with Nong, and then with me. And when Nong crawls into her tent at night, she yells: '*Checkbin? Goodnight!*'

The next day Wichian appears with Si-nuan, as agreed. We spend the entire day together. We negotiate, we talk, we wait, we talk some more, and get to know each other a little better. I am almost beginning to like him, this flirtatious mahout.

Elephants are an integral part of Wichian's family, they have always had six or seven of them. For generations, the mahout knowledge has been passed on from father to son. Wichian regrets that the animals have become a commodity, he longs for the old days. But he also makes a profit from buying and selling them, as well.

He has two children, a thirteen-year-old girl and a nine-year-old boy. His son is already learning the tricks of the trade, but Wichian doesn't want him to be a mahout. A good education, that's what his children should have. 'But my son doesn't want to go to school, he likes elephants much better.' Can you blame him? To children, a mahout is a hero, even more impressive than our train engine driver. Experienced mahouts know better. Today, the profession has hit rock bottom, many a mahout writes down 'driver' when asked about his profession. Moreover, it is a hard existence. 'Begging is increasingly difficult,' Wichian says. 'It's hazardous to enter the city, you get arrested at once. The villages are not as strict, but there you can't earn as much. That's why we have to keep moving around.'

During the dry period after the Surin festival, they usually travel in groups of about six elephants and up to fifteen people. From a central base camp, they travel to the surrounding villages. 'I don't like this life, and it's absolutely bad for my elephants. But if I don't do it, they will starve. I'd rather own land, to be able to grow enough food.' There are a number of ceremonies in Surin in March and April, in which elephants play an important part, and where the mahouts can make some money. After that, in the rainy season, the elephants can stay in Surin. Everything starts to grow, and there is plenty to eat.

Wichian is a true son of Ban Tha Klang. Before he leaves for the city with Si-nuan, he always performs a ceremony to predict whether the trip will be favourable. Just as in the old days, when shamans went elephant hunting. 'We cook a chicken, and pick out its jaw bone. When it is bent, prospects are unfavourable. When it is very much bent, we stay at home.' He also takes a handful of dirt from the village with him, to protect him from evil.

But besides being a son of his village, he is also a child of the times. Six thousand euros for Si-nuan? Can it be seven? We stick to our offer. Halfway through the day, we close the deal, and everybody is relieved. But at the animal district office, spirits drop to zero when we find that the computers don't work due to a power failure. 'Please come back on Monday,' the civil servant keeps saying, but he doesn't know all the setbacks we have overcome so far, how hard it was to come to an agreement with Wichian, that even now he threatens to leave if things are not settled right away. I am about to lose my temper. 'They didn't even use a computer last time,' I desperately yell at Lee, 'why don't you tell that official to use a pen!' Lee snaps that I should keep out of it. Become friends, I know, stay friendly, pretend to wait together until the computers are back on line, bring up interesting topics, but never ever get angry. Lee talks and talks, sends out Yut to make copies, and finally convinces the civil servant to use the good old-fashioned ballpoint pen. It's a narrow escape, but at exactly four o'clock the document has all the prescribed signatures. The office closes. Wichian counts the money. He can smile again and keeps casting impertinent looks at my legs.

I ask him what he will do with the money. 'Buy a new tractor,' he says. We go for a drink to clinch the bargain. Wichian is talkative. He tells us that the real training at the Elephant Study Centre is done by mahouts who are connected to the centre, but who do the training at home, out of sight. Thus they avoid monitoring and are able to earn a little extra. For example, if someone wants to teach his elephant a trick, he can hire Wichian. 'What are the most popular tricks?' I want to know. 'Sitting up with front legs in the air, playing the harmonica, dancing, and greeting.' Wichian calls himself a training expert. Nung Ning was seven months old when he took her away from Si-nuan and schooled her to be a circus performer. When he sold her, she already knew all the tricks, that's why her price was so high. I think: how strange then for her to be so unruly over in Phang Nga. But I don't say so.

He shows us how he taught Nung Ning to sit. He gives the sit command and uses two hooks on the back to push her haunches to the ground, then one hook under her front legs to pull them up. 'Pain is important, she'll remember it. When she is in the correct position, she is given food.' This he repeats until she just needs the command. The harmonica lessons consist of wedging the instrument in the trunk and poking her with something sharp if she lets go. It takes about a week to make it sound acceptable.

For a young elephant, dancing must be even more unpleasant than for a Dutch navvy. The front feet are tied together and the elephant has to stand on the back legs. When she is poked in the flanks and tries to move away from the pain, this results in movements that faintly resemble dancing. Poking different body parts brings on different 'dances'.

I ask Wichian if he has ever participated in a hunt. 'We're leaving soon for Laos to get elephants, do you want to join us?' He is going to a camp where trained elephants are on offer. Probably recently caught in the wild. He doesn't volunteer more details, I should just come along. 'Can girls be mahouts?' I ask. 'You bet! Come and live with us in Tha Klang for a while, I can teach you. I'm the best trainer around. I just got me a lovely sweet new elephant, seven years old!'

We go and get the truck we also used to transport Dok-ngeon, and park it at Wichian's house. Si-nuan walks majestically over to us, Wichian on her back. The sun is low, the children are quiet, the bent-backed village elderly have taken front row seats to watch the proceedings. Wichian and his wife wash Si-nuan for the last time. All family members bless her by pouring a bowl of water over her. They apologise to her for everything they have done wrong, wish her a good journey, and a good life.

In the truck, I am waiting with Lee. Si-nuan gets in calmly. When she spots the bags of bananas and melons we brought, she seems to forget her surroundings. 'First you will spend some time with the nice Madee family,' I say to her. 'Then we'll set out for the Park. You won't have to beg along the road, we won't even go into the city. People will come to admire you and to give you food. Soon you will meet Dok-ngeon, you'll have to take care of her a little, because she's younger than you. We went looking for your baby in Phuket; I'm very sorry, she's dead. But soon, at the Park, you'll see lots of new babies, and maybe one of them will pick you as its aunt.'

Again, I'm in the luggage compartment at the back of the cabin, in front of Si-nuan's head. With her one eye she checks the road, first one side, then the other. Right next to me she opens her mouth wide to feel the wind. It must be a strange sensation for this slow moving animal to hurtle along the motorway at forty miles an hour. With her trunk she sniffs my legs and my face. The moon rises. Now I have two elephants on my conscience.

7

Singing Songs

WE HAVE FIVE days left in Chiang Mai to take care of transportation and residence permits, because all animal offices close between Christmas and New Year. Lee has spelled it out for me: Mae Taeng has approved the arrival of the elephants. Now Surin has to give permission for departure, and grant a transportation permit for the trip to Ayutthaya. Then, Ayutthaya has to agree with this, communicate to Surin that we have arrived, and grant a transportation permit for the trip to Lopburi. After a week they have to communicate that we have left, etcetera, etcetera. Finally, Mae Taeng has to tell all the offices that we have arrived and that the elephants have officially been registered. In these five days, copies of every document—Si-nuan's and Dokngeon's identification papers, sale and ownership certificates—have to be sent to all the animal offices. Then we have to call to make sure they have arrived. Lee has to get back to Surin to finalise the transportation permits. And since he is going there anyway, Lek says, he can also take care of the sale of Malai Thong, the Madee family's crippled elephant, and rent a truck to take her back to Chiang Mai. Lee smiles bravely and says: 'I'll do my best.'

On the day of departure he comes running into the office all sweaty. He has all the paperwork with him in a folder: contact data for three temples and three schools, the identification papers of the elephants, the documents of the previous owners, his own identity card, Lek's identity card and her contract, documents from the Elephant Nature Park, the permit from Mae Taeng, a letter from Doctor Nit, the vet who will accompany us, numbers of the roads we will take, the truck driver's identity card, and the licence plate of the truck. 'I just need more money. Where is the mahout? Is the truck ready?' Miraculously, at the very last moment everything seems to have been taken care of. Lee manages to scatter all his papers over the floor, picks them up, gets the last of the money and runs off.

At the office of Lek's travel agency, everybody works for *Bring the elephant home* this week. Interns translate our English texts into Thai, tap them into the computer, and print leaflets. The graphic designers make posters. Oi buys bright red T-shirts and has the logo printed on them. Doctor Nit stocks up on medicine for the elephants and the mobile animal clinic. Pom picks the two young mahouts, Narong and Wiset, to join our tour. Lek takes care of the truck. Nong buys kitchenware and some basic ingredients. Yut departs for the market with a grocery list of things he has to try and come by cheaply. I take four helpers to a wholesale business in camping supplies. Everybody is enthusiastically loading carts, while I, Checkbin to the core, protest at every item because it's too expensive. In the end, the tents, blankets, inflatable beds, pans, plates, cutlery, and lighting only cost 160 euros. While we are loading the stuff into the van, Lee calls. The transportation permits are in order, he and Malai Thong are on their way to Chiang Mai.

We don't want to miss that, so we head for the Park. You'd think Malai Thong could use some peace and quiet after sixteen hours of relentless truck travel, but after her dinner she immediately hobbles towards the river on her crippled foot, to where the other elephants are. She visits every family to make their acquaintance and stands in the middle of the bustle, trunks touching her from all sides. They seem to like her. Old lady Lilly, who is usually not that interested in other elephants, follows Malai Thong like a teenager in love. Malai Thong could use a wise friend, since she is only twenty-five and handicapped to boot. When I saw her at the Surin festival four weeks ago, compulsively swaying back and forth, I hadn't thought her to be so sociable and friendly. After her bath, she walks into a field with a group. Will this be her new family? What a reception! I can hardly wait for Si-nuan and Dok-ngeon to walk into the Park and be welcomed by the herd.

∗∗∗

We leave at seven o'clock in the evening: Yut, Nong, Narong, Wiset, Lee, Hanna, and I. Doctor Nit will join us in Ayutthaya. We are on the road for sixteen hours. Early on Christmas Day, we park the car in front of the Madee family's house, where Dok-ngeon and Si-nuan are staying. Duang, the almost sixty-year-old head of the family, has been watching them day and night from a makeshift tent, on the harvested rice field where they are with his own elephant.

When Duang and his wife hear we want to stay here for a week, they are worried. Is their house good enough for us? No problem, I say, we don't want to cause you any trouble at all, we'll stay with the elephants. Duang looks at me as if I had made him an indecent proposal, he believes we should stay at the village. Yut and Nong look happy, since as true city dwellers they don't appreciate camping too much. At least the village has running water and electricity. But I am unyielding, at the very least I want to explore the camping possibilities.

The only suitable place turns out to be along the path near the field, between a row of skinny eucalyptus trees. After some arguing, Yut and Nong give in. At least there's a more or less clean stream passing nearby, and the mini-van can make it there, so we won't have to drag stuff across the field all the time. Everything is all right for me, because the elephants are grazing in front of our camp.

While we are unpacking, Duang takes his moped to fetch his wife, Yan. She has to see this, no way she should miss this! The folding picnic table with benches attached is mercilessly laughed at. But I love our camp. Surrounding the small kitchen with the charcoal burners are six blue tents. Beneath a plastic sheet, we create a chill-out place with lots of pillows, and strung up between the eucalyptus trees is the banner, in English and in Thai: *Bring the elephant home.* We all hang up the Christmas decorations together while singing Jingle Bells. Nong serves Christmas dinner. *Kaeng khieo-wan taohu,* hot green curry with little aubergines, tofu, and coconut. There's not a restaurant where this would have tasted better. There's also tempura, a pineapple stuffed with curry *phanaeng,* a mushroom salad, *tom-yam* soup, and for dessert sweet, sticky rice with mango and coconut cream. I deliver an inspiring speech in honour of our first milestone. The word team is often mentioned, and when I'm finished there is loud applause and laughter, and toasts with pints of Chang beer. *Chok di,* good luck! We exchange Christmas presents; Lee has a Buddhist good luck necklace for everyone. They are made of pieces of temple bells a hundred years old. When I put it around my neck, power seems to emanate from it.

When I open the zipper of my tent in the morning, I see Si-nuan and Dok-ngeon together in the field in front of our camp. How often haven't I dreamt of this? The experience is almost unreal. Duang brings us drinking water. We are lucky to have him around. Wiset and Narong are hesitant in their dealings with the elephants, they do not yet have authority over them, and only Duang seems to really be in control. He always carries his goad, but I never see him using it to beat or poke. He also lends it to Wiset and Narong, who don't seem to be bothered by it at all. Duang teaches Wiset, who will be Dok-ngeon's mahout, how to disinfect her head wound, and how to remove the puss. Duang also reassures Si-nuan when Narong mounts her. At some moment, Dok-ngeon sneaks off into the field. Slowly at first, then she takes to her heels. Three mahouts go after her. '*How! How!*' they call in unison, 'Stop!' But she runs around like mad and will only calm down when she finds Wiset in front of her. It worries me. This is not an option when we're surrounded by a hundred schoolchildren!

We have no running water and no toilet at the camp. The eucalyptus trees don't provide a lot of privacy, so every now and then we take the mini-van to a nearby gas station that has a squat toilet and a tap. With towels, soap, and toilet paper, and the Thai superstar Bird on the CD-player, we merrily drive over to our sanitary oasis. Pouring clean water on your head feels like pure luxury.

Our Thai team members always have a hot breakfast, usually with the left-overs from the previous day. No matter how much we love Thai food, Hanna and I want bread in the morning. We toast the white mealy squares over a charcoal fire and put jam on them. Sometimes we find slices of cheese in a supermarket, and although they taste like socks, we love them. After breakfast, we wash some bananas and walk over to the elephants. Dok-ngeon is always the first one there, she runs towards us and gobbles up as much as she can. We sneak around her to supply Si-nuan, but she usually comes after us. '*How, how!*' we call out our newly learned elephant command.

It's not just at Christmas time that Nong goes all out in her kitchen. Every meal—lunch and dinner—consists of at least six different dishes, in vegetarian and non-vegetarian versions. In his normal life, Lee does eat meat, but now he has decided to join Hanna and me. Yut helps Nong with the cooking and shopping. Everything we eat is fresh from the market.

In the afternoon, we hang out in the camp, take pictures for the website, write the newsletter, and answer e-mails on the laptop. We also develop the school programme for the tour. At the end of the afternoon, we often take a walk through the cooling fields into the village to surf the Internet and buy fresh bananas. On one of our last days, I send out sixty press releases to the Thai media, and get an immediate response. I make an appointment for an interview with *The Nation*, one of the two major English daily newspapers in Thailand.

In the evening, the elephants get their medicine. Four penicillin pills for Dok-ngeon, two for Si-nuan, hidden in a bunch of bananas. It is a bit scary to go looking for the elephants in the dark. Once, Lee almost stepped on a snake. They scare me to death. Wearing our flip-flops, we walk in line across the rice stubble. Narong thinks my fear of snakes is funny, so suddenly he screams 'snake' and runs after me. Maybe we should wear shoes and socks, next time around.

When all the work is done, we often play games with Wiset and Narong. Hangman is a favourite, we each take turns chalking the figure on the little blackboard we have bought for the school programme. It is dark by seven o'clock and we go to bed earlier and earlier, even before nine o'clock. There are countless stars, the nights are quiet. Except for that one night when mopeds race noisily past our camp. Next day, Lee goes to investigate. It seems some mahouts are enraged, because we are campaigning against begging with elephants. We decide here is not the place to hand out the leaflets we have made.

***

Our field lies between two villages, Ban Ta Lat and Ban Moi. The latter is the Madee family's village. There are a number of stone houses, but Duang's house, at the far end of the village, is made of wood. Almost all the houses are raised on stilts. At ground level, hens peck around, traps and nets are hung up, and there are large jars, barrels, and tanks in which rainwater is collected. There is usually a big low table on which—shoes off!—you can sit. The upper part of the house is shut, that's where the family sleeps. The village has only a few small shops. It seems most people have to get by on little money.

We invite the Madee family to dinner on New Year's Eve. They bring their four grandchildren, two girls and two boys. Their parents have taken the elephants to beg, grandma and grandpa are taking care of the grandchildren. Nong serves all kinds of shellfish, it's a feast. The family has brought us organic rice, a famous produce of Surin, and invites us to the village party that night. When every dish has been scraped clean, we inflate heaps of balloons to take with us, and pack everybody and the balloons into the mini-van. Narong jumps on the moped with Duang. Upon arrival at the village square, I am the first one to get out of the van, still working on the balloons. Suddenly four speakers are blaring simultaneously: *'Farang ma laeo! Farang ma laeo!'* The foreigners are

Fig 29. Girl mahout Ploy

Fig 30. Pa Keao (photo: Antoinette van de Water)

Fig 31. Duang, Si-nuan, and Narong near Wat Mongkhon Prasit, Lopburi

Fig 32. Narong rides on Si-nuan to a primary school in Lopburi

Fig 33. 'Making merit' by giving offerings to monks

Fig 34. Nuns feed Dok-ngeon at Wat Mongkhon Prasit

Fig 35. Former location of elephant stables in King Narai's palace

Fig 36. Monks bring temple dogs to the mobile animal clinic

Fig 37. Docter Nit castrates dogs during the school programme in Lopburi

Fig 38. Clockwise, from the left: Duang, Wiset, Nachon, Ford, Oey, Nong, and Yut

Fig 39. *Khit thueng . . .*

Fig 40. Elephant shaman Boonma and his colleagues, Surin

Fig. 41. Photo opportunity: police and shamans, Surin

Fig 42. On the way to Sukhothai, Duang keeps the elephants company

here already! When I look up, I see a hundred pairs of eyes focused on me. I leap back into the van and yell: 'Everybody is looking at me!' After being heartily laughed at, I still have to get back out, where I take a deep bow.

Fortunately, I don't have to go on stage right away. We all get to sample a local brew. The villagers have set up a party area for games and presentations. After a few hours of these it's our turn. Hanna and I get up on the stage, thank the village for its hospitality, and praise the party profusely. It's not enough, we have to sing a song. Like the true-blue Dutchies that we are, we are tongue-tied. Then the *Chang* song comes to mind. '*Chang chang chang . . .*', the first words are easy, but what follows is increasingly off-key and confused. No wonder the audience wants to hear a Dutch song as well. We can't come up with anything but the Dutch translation of the *Chang* song, which turns out to be just as embarrassing as the Thai version. Right then and there I decide that we have to learn a good Dutch song as quickly as possible for future events.

The host has one last question: what do we think of the party? Hanna calls out the first words that come to mind with great enthusiasm: '*Aroi mak mak!*' Very tasty! Something we say to Nong at every meal. The villagers go quiet. Everybody is watching us very seriously. Except for Yut and Nong, who are overcome with laughter at their table at the back. Someone whispers: '*Sanuk mak mak!*' '*Sanuk mak mak*,' Hanna says cheerfully into the microphone. Relief, everybody laughs and applauds. And then we can dance. Isan (northeastern) music is the most rhythmic type I have heard in Thailand, it swings and it keeps on going. There's a group of children dancing around us. A beautiful young lady boy with a provocative look beats us all. At eleven o'clock, I check on the rest of the team, who are half asleep and want to go to bed. Nong giggles: '*Taohu, aroi mak mak!*' At midnight I am still awake, five minutes later I have taken off to a dance floor where men are waving bottles of liquor and a baby elephant is shuffling in a strange way.

The next day we are woken up by Lee, who is calling all his girlfriends and relations to wish them a Happy New Year. At least twenty times in a row we hear: '*Sawatdi pi mai*—Happy New Year—*Chang*, Surin, Ayutthaya, Lopburi, Sukhothai.' Hanna sings after him: 'Ayutthaya, Lopburi, Sukhothai', a cheerful magic spell. Oh yes, we are on our way! We fold leaflets, everybody lends a hand, even Duang. He carefully reads the Thai text, nods every now and again, then starts over again. He looks up with his wonderful, broad smile. It means a lot to me, the approval of this experienced mahout. I jump for joy when he announces he wants to join our tour. He is curious about the Elephant Nature Park and wants to see how his handicapped elephant Malai Thong is faring. We have gained another team member.

I try hard to come up with a Dutch song to make sure that in the future we are spared the embarrassment of last night. I vaguely remember a song about a dinosaur, what if I change it a little? 'I am a little elephant, I wander through the woods, usually I wear a leash, today I can go free! O yes, o yes, o yes, o yes, o yeeeeeeeees!' A song with hit potential, I notice when Narong is able to bellow along enthusiastically after hearing it just once. When we are tidying up the camp, the truck arrives for the elephants, and brings another three new team members. Driver Nachon has brought his wife Oey and toddler Ford. When everybody is in the tents, Nong calls: 'Ayutthaya!' From the other tents comes: 'Lopburi, Sukhothai! Good night!'

On Friday we get up at five thirty. Everybody is wearing their temple bell necklaces and a red T-shirt with our logo. Packing up proceeds like clockwork. Dok-ngeon is eating bananas, Si-nuan checks out the truck. When Nachon starts the engine, she takes off. Duang runs after her and sprains his ankle. 'Narong, *pai, pai!*' he yells, go, go! But Narong gives up quickly. Lee grabs some bunches of bananas and jumps into the field. He returns with Si-nuan like a hero. Angry too; of course this must never happen again. What if one of the elephants breaks into a run on the temple grounds where we'll be camping?

The sun rises, the field looks like a fairy-tale. Getting the elephants into the truck is no problem at all. For the first time, they are standing quietly side by side in the back of the white truck, that has our banner on the side. In front of them and at their rear, round beams have been slotted in to hold, support, and help them keep their balance. I am in the luggage compartment at the back of the cabin. Duang and Wiset are in the back of the truck. I feed the elephants pineapples and bananas, but Si-nuan can smell that the bags I'm sitting on contain even more treats, and uses her mighty trunk to get to them. She gets hold of one of the bags. I try to swap a cucumber for it, while trying not to fall off, since the road is very bumpy. It is a heroic fight, but in the end Si-nuan has eaten all the cucumbers and I get the empty bag back. As luck would have it, I turn around and see an electricity cable approaching: duck! A decapitation on the first leg of the journey might be a bad omen. The remainder of the trip I sit between Lee and Nachon in the cabin.

It gets very hot in the afternoon. When we pass the first police post, Lee explains we only have to stop when there is also a branch of the animal office. That occurs only once. Lee gets a stamp and we can continue. The good luck necklaces work.

8

Initiations

IN AYUTTHAYA, THREE rivers meet, the Chao Phraya, the Lopburi, and the Pasak. No wonder this city was an economic and political centre in past times. In 1350, a Thai ruler began construction, and it was soon the seat of successive dynasties until 1767, when the Burmese made a devastating attack.

The present-day city still has many features testifying to the grand past. There are ancient canals where now large black rice barges are towed by elegant tugboats. Remnants of five hundred Buddhist monasteries have been found, but also of mosques, Hindu sanctuaries, and Christian churches. Many foreigners were given permission to settle in Ayutthaya, among them Dutch merchants. Thailand has welcomed foreign influence from time to time. Maybe that's why it has never been colonised, as neighbouring countries have. When you can get access to a country's riches through trade, why try to conquer it?

The historic buildings stand more or less together in the old part of the city. They are walled-in, lush areas that are nice places to visit, especially in the evening. The sun goes down beyond the crumbling towers. Some look like large bells and are called *chedi*, others vaguely resemble corncobs and are called *prang*. In the ruins of the ancient palaces, ghosts of whispering courtiers in sparkling gowns drift past, they dart off between the pillars, and silently climb the steep stairways. The signs speak of kings and battles for the throne, the buildings speak of sacred architecture and Buddha. Back then, no one had heard of the separation of state and religion.

The majority of the buildings are constructed of large flat oblong bricks plastered over. It's strange to think how all these round shapes are made of oblongs on the inside. I am reminded of the Spaarndammer Buurt in Amsterdam, where the architects of the Amsterdam School have sculpted with bricks in the same festive way. Here, even the larger statues of Buddha have been constructed in this fashion, while the smaller ones have been carved from natural stone. Almost all the heads are missing. Has there been an oriental iconoclasm here? Only torsos remain, seated with crossed legs, hands upturned on their laps. Signs warn tourists not to have their pictures taken posing with their head in the empty spot.

Wat Pa Keao, the temple where we are allowed to set up camp is right next to a canal, on the edge of town near a collection of houses which we would call a suburb and here is called a village. Wat Pa Keao functions fully in the here and now, and the main building is boringly modern. The fact that *prang* and *chedi* are missing is normal, they are a thing of the past. But this temple also lacks pointed roofs, curly decorations, and sparkling glass mosaics, it doesn't look like the Thai temples I know. Wat Pa Keao is an ungainly white building on concrete pillars, almost Dutch in its plainness. It doesn't matter, we're quite happy to be welcome here, and to have our elephants stay on the grounds at night. During the day, the mahouts take them to an undeveloped piece of land down the road.

Si-nuan and Dok-ngeon are upset, no wonder after the bumpy ride. '*Bong*,' Duang says, 'Drink!', but they wave their trunks listlessly, and it takes them a while to become elephants again instead of cattle in transport. Their paddock isn't exactly 'back to nature' either. An elephant researcher once told me that at the national park where he worked, a 103 different kinds of elephant food-plants had been found. This pasture only has grass and water, and is neighbour to a company called 'Brassieres Twin Peaks'. Behind it, next to a slum, is a residential neighbourhood with a barrier and security guards.

We put up our tents close to the white temple, but have to relocate almost right away. Fleas! The area between the pillars appears to be a refuge for the many dogs that hang around here. People often bring stray animals and discarded pets to temples, where monks will feed them. The dogs and cats here, besides being half wild and nervous, have strange growths and skin diseases. Doctor Nit has her work cut out for her.

We all go to the market in the city at nightfall. Nong, Oey, Yut, and Nachon immediately disappear among the booths. I buy some beer and *The Nation*, the newspaper that interviewed me. Bingo! A big, positive story, with pictures. The first Thai media offensive has produced results.

'There's no fruit for the elephants,' Yut reports, 'too expensive here.' 'Did you look everywhere, did you tell them it's for the elephants, did you try to get the price down? If we have to, we'll pay more. They really need power food right now.' Yut sighs and follows me across the market again, grumbling. Actually, he is right, it is expensive here. So, that's how it has to be. I buy some bunches of bananas. Ridiculous, says Yut.

Back at Wat Pa Kaeo, the gas burners and charcoal fires are lit and the spoils from the market are transformed into some eight fragrant dishes. Damien, a French photo-journalist, joins us for dinner tonight. He is working on a book about the relationship between man and animal in Thailand. Just like me, he is surprised about the combination of respect and cruelty. He talks about the city of Lopburi, our next port of call. Lopburi is known for its monkeys. Originally there was a group of macaques at the temple of the Hindu god Kala. Monkeys are considered to be the children of Kala. It is bad luck to harm them, so the group could procreate without any disturbance. When a dominant male chose the inviting city over life at the temple, half the group followed him. This gang is now prowling around Lopburi; they break off car antennae, break windows, and steal food wherever they can.

Damien says tourists overfeed the temple monkeys to such a degree that they have become extremely picky. Someone noticed how they would only eat the yolks of eggs, after which poor people would grab the discarded egg whites. The fat temple monkeys chase away the skinny ones that linger around town, and the animals have by now become such a plague that the people of Lopburi drive them off with catapults.

This is of course a great subject for urban legend, but there is one story Damien has witnessed himself. People believe 'you can increase your chances for a good reincarnation by paying for the cremation of a dead monkey,' he says. 'When someone offered us this opportunity, I said that in that case a monkey had to die first. Oh no, there were plenty of bodies in cold storage!' There is an abundance of 'good deeds' like this performed in Thailand. Like releasing birds, as I saw in Chiang Mai. 'Or releasing tortoises,' Damien says. 'Only with them you can be absolutely sure that they are picked up again after you have left.'

**

Seven o'clock in the morning, the sun dances through the smoke clouds rising from the mahouts' fire. Lee is already sweeping leaves, children in uniform walk hand in hand to the school next to the temple. I fish out my toilet bag and towel from my bag, and climb the stairs to the far end of the temple hall, where there are real showers and real toilets. Luxury!

On this first day we do the groundwork. We hang our large banner and three large elephant posters. In front of them, we set out some tables with leaflets, and decorate everything with table cloths and lights. Lee arranges a boat for us to go and buy elephant food in the market on the other bank of the canal, and goes to the animal office himself, along with Doctor Nit. He returns smiling broadly: we have permission for the transport to Lopburi, and tomorrow an officer will come over to take care of the documents. He has also talked to the headmaster of the primary school next to the temple, and we are welcome to visit tomorrow. Suddenly I get nervous. Three hundred Thai kids . . . Come on, Antoinette, I try to reassure myself, the Theresia School in Rotterdam was a success, wasn't it?

We go looking for the village chief. An authoritative looking man is fixing his son's bike in the yard of the house. A blinding white smile, all friendliness. Certainly we can set up the animal clinic here, certainly we can announce the campaign, wonderful even! This business with street elephants should be stopped, it's a disgrace. We can get a car and megaphones to drive around the district—no, we misunderstood, we can go on local radio tonight! Mr. Chaiyapan Fuengkanjanakul is not the village chief, but managing director and host of Radio Ayutthaya 93.75 FM. We are expected to report at the studio at six thirty tonight.

By the evening the bush telegraph seems to have worked quite well, even without electronic devices. Dozens of inquisitive villagers are visiting our camp. The elephants are the stars, completely according to plan. Si-nuan strips the leaves from a palmfrond stem, and then snaps it. 'Oooohhhhh!' the public calls out when Dok-ngeon uses her leg to break a whole banana tree trunk in half. A flap-eared boy of about eight years old just stands and stares. He devours the elephants with his eyes. Then he approaches Si-nuan, holds out his hand and touches everything within reach. A life-time experience, for sure. Later on we see him stripping banana leaves from their spines with all his strength, rather like Si-nuan.

I find it a little scary, all these children so close to the elephants. Si-nuan cannot see on one side, so if someone suddenly pulls her tail, she can get angry and then . . . I have to stop the film playing in my head, and ask Wiset and Narong to keep a close eye on things, when Lee and I proceed to the local radio station for the broadcast.

It is getting dark. The sign saying 93.75 FM is almost as big as the building. The radio relies entirely on volunteers, says Mr. Chaiyapan Fuengkanjanakul. They broadcast the entire day, whenever there is news they go on air. The broadcasts can be heard on the radio at home and from speakers in the street, in Ayutthaya and in twelve communities around it.

In a glass booth filled with switches and slides, we meet the deejay and hostess, the twelve-year-old niece of the director. 'Miss Thanaporn,' he introduces her. She pulls the switches and manipulates the slides, bends over the microphone, and we are on air. It is a relaxed conversation, we get all the time we need to tell about what it is we do, and why. We announce the animal clinic and the school programme. We talk about Si-nuan and Dok-ngeon, and about the Elephant Nature Park. An ancient king looks down in approval from his frame on the wall behind us. Afterwards we swap our red T-shirts with our logo for shiny blue ones with 93.75 FM on them. Hanna and I put them on for the inevitable group picture and look like rugby-groupies.

***

In preparation for the school programme we rehearse the Thai and Dutch elephant songs after breakfast. 'O yeeeees, o yeeeees!' Nong sings along. At nine thirty, we spot two lilac caterpillars crawling our way. Two lines of little children in purplish-pink uniforms, their hands on each other's shoulders, as if dancing the conga. An unscheduled visit from the kindergarten. 'Camera standby!' Lee calls. 'Do we have small eat for children?' Fortunately, we had thrown all our health principles overboard yesterday, and stocked up on bags of crisps and candy. Apparently they're not the children's first crisps and candy; out of every ten children at least one is overweight, and many teeth show signs of sugar overdose.

Lee feels like a fish in the water. He loves acting and he loves children, it makes him the perfect elephant show master. That he brackets Holland together with tulips and windmills, oh well, Akzo and the IJsselmeer Dam might be a little complicated for four- and five-year-olds. We needn't have bothered to practice the Thai elephant song. Before Lee can even say it, the children burst into singing: '*Chang chang chang . . .*' And again, '*Chang chang chang . . .*'

Because of the school programme, Si-nuan and Dok-ngeon haven't been taken to their pasture today, they are still at our camp. It's an unfair competition for Lee, his educational story about elephants against the living examples under the trees. He quickly switches to the next part of the programme, 'group pictures with the elephants'. After that, the teachers line the children up, boys with boys and girls with girls, and the lilac caterpillars crawl back to school. In the meantime, Doctor Nit has arranged all the paperwork with the animal officer, who has quietly arrived. He's doing it for free. From this moment on I don't have to worry about permits anymore, that millstone is taken from my neck.

Lee gets a call from an acquaintance in Surin. The government wants to start paying mahouts a salary, provided they stay home with their elephants and don't come begging in the cities anymore. I have read about this before, in the *Bangkok Post*, and recover the article from a folder. It dates from late 2005, and it says: 'Surin revives New World for Elephant Project'. The cabinet has given the go-ahead to a local initiative that intends to set up an elephant shelter, pay mahouts eight thousand baht a month, reforest two areas near the shelter, and build houses for the mahouts. Three hundred and fifty of the one thousand registered mahouts with house elephants have already signed on, and the government has budgetted 600 million baht, according to the article.

On January 8, says Lee's acquaintance, this programme will be festively introduced in Ban Tha Klang, the heart of elephant country. Mahouts are invited to come and register, there will be an elephant buffet, and the prime minister will open the festivities. Supposedly there are about two hundred elephants in and around the village already. January 8, that's in two days, can we make it? We can, Lee says. But we'll have to drive at night, because the programme starts at six o'clock in the morning, with offerings to the monks. A perfect opportunity to 'make merit'. And where merit can be made, Lee is present. I think he has a secret longing for the monastery, our manager.

Around noon we hang our campaign materials in the large open-air hall of the primary school next to the temple. From the classrooms next to it, old-fashioned choruses escape, it sounds like a collective practice of multiplication tables. Plastic chairs are set up in rows with military precision by teachers who have donned their best shirts. Here come the children. Fortunately not three hundred of them, but still at least a hundred. The boys are wearing white-and-brown uniforms, the girls white-and-blue. When they take off their shoes, as is common practise in Thailand, plenty of socks appear to have holes. Most of the children come from villages in the area, the lady principal says. Poor families, often without a father.

An expectant buzz fills the hall, as if Santa Claus is about to make an appearance. Our entire team is present, wearing red T-shirts. To an outsider we must present a peculiar sight. The tough mahouts Narong, Duang, and Wiset, the city folk Yut and Nong, the respectable Doctor Nit, Lee wearing his camouflage trousers, and two nervous girls from Holland. Okay, here we go. 'I am a little elephant, I wander through the woods . . .'

The afternoon is a great success. The elephant quiz turns into a great battle. We put up a rope right across the hall. Lee calls out a question, everybody who thinks the answer is 'yes', jumps over the rope, if 'no' they stay where they are. 'Can an elephant swim?' Immediately half the competitors drop out. 'Does an elephant eat meat?' Pushing, pulling, jumping, jumping back, laughing, tripping, the once so disciplined kids go wild. 'Can an elephant climb a tree?' Unbelievably, twenty children think so. Only later do I understand, when I see an elephant happily walk up a tree trunk in a TV commercial. And that is nothing compared to the commercial where elephants in suits are sitting behind computers. 'Does an elephant snore?' There are four winners left.

The English class is a success, in the form of games with words like 'elephant' and 'tusk'. It's nothing new for the kids; English is already taught at primary school. The children have to learn two different alphabets right away, which can't be easy.

Finally, we ask the children to make elephant drawings. After they turn them in, we will pick the best ones, and the winners get prizes. We hand out pens and notebooks to all of the kids. In consultation with the headmaster, six students have been picked to whom we give a small amount of money for school supplies. 'Poor children who are doing well,' the headmaster has assured us. We put in a T-shirt as well. I do think it's a little embarrassing, this charity. But I believe I should follow Lee in this. He knows what's proper.

At the end of the day, the children invade our camp. They have brought bananas and sugar cane for Si-nuan and Dok-ngeon, and a boy has brought his new notebook along to draw Si-nuan. Duang is watching him and shaking his head. 'Those ears have to be smaller, this is an African elephant!' A little further on children swamp Narong with questions. 'Why are Si-nuan's ears so big?' Narong explains this improves hearing, and that she flares them sometimes to impress the other elephants. 'And when the wind blows along her ears, the whole elephant cools down.' 'How fast can she walk?' 'Up to twenty-five miles per hour.' 'I'm going to ask my father to buy two elephants, too!' A fat boy doesn't leave Narong's side. His name is Kirk. 'Like the American movie star.' He will sleep in Narong's tent that night and every following night in Ayutthaya. He has found his hero. The woman who took us to the market in her boat yesterday visits again, with ten banana trees and her baby, whom she proudly holds up in the air. Hanna throws a frisbee with a group of children next to the temple. We're an elephant playground.

The next morning Doctor Nit shows her skills for the first time. At eight o'clock the monks usually feed all the cats and dogs that wander around the temple grounds, so it is a good opportunity to treat them. We catch ten of them, with difficulty. I put on a pair of plastic gloves and apply myself to smearing bald spots and rashes with pink ointment from a large jar. Doctor Nit injects antibiotics, vitamins, and a remedy for fleas and ticks. Open wounds are being disinfected with the same purple stuff that is used for the elephants. Next, we move to the school hall we used yesterday, a cool place where many dogs hang out. Here we treat some more of the pitiful creatures. People drop by with their pets, I am relieved to see they look fairly healthy, like the dog balanced between husband and wife on a moped. When Doctor Nit comes at him with her needles, the poor animal is shaking and whining. After three shots he is in shock, but when he realises it's over, he jumps up onto his mistress's lap on the back of the moped. They drive off as happy customers.

We have to move our tents at the end of the morning. There will be a celebration in the temple hall. 'It is a public area,' Lee says. 'Everybody can use it, you only have to pay for electricity and water. The abbot told me that today families will be saying goodbye to their sons who will become monks.' And with a big smile: 'No more sex from now on!'

We have hardly even packed up our tents, when the first heavily loaded trucks enter the grounds, and within half an hour Thai pop music can be heard far and wide. 'Strange,' Lee says with a look of disapproval. 'That's not like the monks. And they have beer as well.' Many monks are not observing the rules as they should, he explains. He prefers the forest monks. 'Very strict, very good! They withdraw in the woods, they don't drink alcohol and don't smoke. They eat only once a day, and only the food they gather with their begging bowl.

They mix everything together, it doesn't matter what it is. But values are fading. There are fewer young monks, too, these days.'

Lek calls. She has bought two elephants, a mother and a three-day-old baby. The mother was forced to keep working at a trekking camp during her pregnancy—which lasts about twenty-two months—and the baby was born prematurely. It's great that more animals have been rescued. Within two months, five elephants join the herd: Malai Thong, bought by Lek in Surin, Si-nuan and Dok-ngeon, and now these two. But we really have to find funds to expand the grounds.

In the afternoon I cycle on my rented bike—far too small, built for somebody of Thai size—into town. Internet cafe, update the website, answer mail. There are at least fifty e-mails and two extensive letters of application, those I pass on to Eric, our representative in Holland. I need to go to the Elephant Palace.

***

I had noticed it on the city map: Elephant Palace and Royal Kraal. 'Kraal' is a word that is central in Thai elephant history. Unlike the Suai in Surin, who caught elephants from the back of their own elephant using a rope made of buffalo hide, other groups organised drives that ended in a kraal, an extremely strong enclosure. This way, dozens of elephants were captured simultaneously. The Royal Kraal in Ayutthaya still exists, now part of a tourist attraction.

When I get close, elephants walk towards and past me, beautifully dressed in red and yellow silk, as are their mahouts. They carry tourists in howdahs, underneath parasols. They are on their way to the temples at the historical park. The Elephant Palace turns out to be a large outdoor stable, where about twenty elephants are waiting to carry tourists. When they return from their hot, dusty trip, they are hosed down with a garden hose. They clearly enjoy it. The atmosphere surrounding the stables is a little like a theme park, with wooden buildings where you can buy souvenirs and soft drinks. There is a young elephant doing tricks, and you can buy bananas to feed to the elephants. Business is good.

And then I see something I haven't seen before: a girl mahout!

Ploy is seventeen. She turns out to be the daughter of the owner. In the morning, she goes to school, in the afternoon she works at the Elephant Palace.

She has been riding elephants since she was six. 'I understand elephants better than people,' she says. 'An elephant can kill you, but he will never lie or cheat. They are my friends, I will stay with them all my life.' When she was eleven, she went to live in New Zealand for three years. Her parents wanted her to learn English. What was it like? 'Boring,' she says, in perfect English. 'I was always indoors. In Thailand you are outside, you can jump into the river if you feel like it, or play with the animals.'

Ploy is the mahout of the young elephant doing tricks in the main stables. 'His name is King Kaeo, he is very smart and tries very hard. When I teach him something, he will have added to it by himself next time. If you want to teach an elephant something, it is important to understand him. You have to watch him carefully, spend a lot of time with him, and do everything together. Sleep, eat, walk, everything.' I ask her if she uses the hooked goad a lot. 'Only when he suddenly runs away, and even then not very often. It is a little like a drunken friend; when he starts to hit people you have to hit him. But why do you ask?' When I explain what it is I do, and mention the name Lek, she frowns. 'Isn't that the lady who made that tape about the *phajaan*? She says it happens everywhere in Thailand, but that isn't true. I don't approve of the *phajaan* either. We don't do that here. We work with rewards, and at the most slap them with the goad.'

Her father, she says, owns 150 elephants. They work partly in the tourist industry in Surin, partly here in Ayutthaya. In the daytime, they carry tourists, at night they go to the Royal Kraal. Next to the enclosure that was the end station of the organised drives of days past, there is a farm where the mahouts and about 50 elephants live together.

'Everybody knows who my father is, he is a well-known business man. Some say he makes money with the elephants, but he doesn't care. He has become rich in other businesses. He loves elephants and doesn't want them to beg in the streets. As long as our elephants are healthy, it's all right.'

We say goodbye. When I get on my bike, I see her eating ice-cream, sitting on King Kaeo's neck. I am a little jealous.

Later on, I find on the Elephant Palace website that about ten thousand tourists take a ride there every year. 'It is somewhat boring but light work for the elephants. It most likely resembles retirement after a life in the treacherous logging industry. Man and animal even get their much-needed day off . . . The Ayutthaya Elephant Camp offers a model to take care of the problems that elephants in Thailand and the rest of the world have to deal with. Without a lot of land, without permanent government support or sponsors, domesticated elephants have to generate an income to survive . . . These diligent workers walk several miles a day across varied terrain, they are among their own sort, and are cared for by a personal companion. The exercise is good for their feet. Their physical and psychological health is further advanced by plenty of healthy food, two baths a day, and supervision by a vet. At night they sleep in a communal area, where they can lie down, communicate, and just be elephants . . . An alternative requires compromises, from elephant as well as man.'

Maybe Ploy's father is right. But if an elephant was given the choice, he would rather be at the Elephant Nature Park, I think.

When I get back to our headquarters, Hanna is enthusiastically going through piles of elephant drawings made by the school children. There are some good likenesses, but also something that looks like an elephant cat, and also one grey block of concrete with a leg at every corner. Elephants near the water, in the forest, in the city, and even on their way from the city to the forest. Elephant dung, including the flies. I have been recorded too, I am standing on a stage putting a bandage on the trunk of an elephant, to my right is a first aid kit, to my left a fruit basket. All the drawings are wonderful, and to my relief the story I have told seems to have hit home. There are a lot of drawings in which elephants are leaving the city and are on their way to a green corner of the paper. After much debate, we pick the winners. We will present the prizes the day after tomorrow, before we leave for Lopburi.

The day's programme concludes with an offering of small scholarships to young monk students at the temple of Wat Pa Keao. Ceremonial gifts are important in Thailand. Everywhere we go, we are given little things. Monks give religious pictures and statues, teachers bring sweets, the headmaster offers us a bunch of bananas. Social interactions over here are much more steeped in decorum than at home. But it's not just to keep up appearances. They create an atmosphere of respect and good will, you can feel it. The ritual is at least as important as the gifts. The bananas are in a nicely decorated basket and they are handed over with an elegant little bow. Perhaps these rituals are a condition for that other side to Thai manners, the informal, the easy-going.

The room where the abbot receives us, is richly decorated as well. Among the Persian rugs, portraits of kings and statues of Buddha, two fragile, ancient monks, a shy student, and the abbot are seated in a cloud of holiness. Everything is in orange, not Dutch soccer orange but sacred orange. After speeches back and forth, I crawl on my knees towards the student, bow, and put the little envelopes with the money on the orange cloth he lays down in front of him. In Holland I wouldn't dream of bowing to a priest, yet here I'm not even troubled by kneeling for a student. We receive amulets with pictures of Buddha.

Outside the Thai pop music that has thundered from the temple hall all day has changed into the meditative sounds of prayer chanting. That's more like it.

***

The next day we immerse ourselves in a Buddhist world again. Lee has arranged for our mobile animal clinic to settle down at Wat Maheyong for a morning. It is a famous temple with a famous abbot. Lee took meditation training there himself.

Wat Maheyong is a little way outside Ayutthaya. We drive into a busy parking area. Plenty of expensive cars, many with foreign licence plates. 'Rich people come from far and wide to hear Phra Khema-rangsi speak,' Lee says. 'The abbot would have preferred to live a life of solitude as a forest monk in a cave, but so many people want to hear him speak, he stays on as a teacher.'

It is a large area, with many buildings, bits of forest, and a water garden. From indoors comes the soothing sound of chanting, rhythmically backed up by hammering and sawing. Construction is going on everywhere, in a traditional style with natural materials. Every now and then, a piece of fairy-tale architecture pops up, like the toilet buildings, disguised as trees. On the edge of the grounds, concrete mixers are churning another load for a cave under construction. 'In Thailand it is no longer easy for a monk to find a cave in the jungle to retreat to,' Lee explains, 'and the existing caves are very remote. That's why they are built here.' Sacred and practical in a cheerful union. It is one of the things that makes Thailand such a wonderful country.

The visitors to the temple are mainly female and dressed in the white clothes of Buddhist nuns, though they differ from them in their fashionable handbags and smart hairdos. The nuns are shaven bald, and busy steering temple proceedings in the right direction. In the middle of the grounds about one hundred visitors are sitting on plastic chairs, waiting for a lecture by Phra Khema-rangsi. He is a tall man, bristly hair above powerful facial features.

Lee softly translates: 'The heart must be healthy. Make your mind only one.' To clarify, he adds: 'He is talking about *jhan*, a condition of concentration on the inner self. There are forty ways to meditate. When you do it right, hours will pass without you knowing it.' The abbot has a deep voice. If an old oak could talk, it probably would sound like this. I submerge in a feeling of peace; suddenly I have all the time in the world, and there are no street elephants to bring home, no funds to raise, no e-mails to answer. Until Lee wakes me from my pleasant stupor. 'Back to work!'

Animals are welcome in Wat Maheyong. Every day a dozen elephants, who work in the tourist industry, stay overnight here, and several times a year the nuns and the monks organise an 'elephant buffet'. Today there is a party for the dogs and cats of the temple because of us. They have a different point of view about this, however, as Lee sadly learns. He picks up one of the dogs to give Doctor Nit the chance to give it an injection. 'Kaikaikai!' the little scared dog barks, and 'snapsnapsnap!' say the other members of her gang. Lee gets two nasty bites in his upper arm and his leg. After that, the nuns take control. Amazing scenes! Two nuns each firmly grab a dog's front leg, the owner of the legs hobbles between them on his hind legs like a toddler who has just learned to walk. One nun has developed the perfect hold for the feared moment when Doctor Nit plants a needle in the dog's behind. She clasps the squealing animal between her calves, with only its head and behind sticking out beyond her white garb and . . . jab! The animals are screaming like piglets and I must admit, when Doctor Nit comes at me while I am holding a puppy in my arms, I shrink back as well. The remainder of the time I am busy with ointments and disinfectants, and mixing worm pills in with dog food. When we leave, Doctor Nit gives a box with animal medicines to the nun in charge of aiding the homeless.

***

The day before moving to Lopburi we spend in Surin, at the celebration of the introduction of the mahout salary. We have driven all night to be on time for the 'making merit ceremony' with the monks. It's six o'clock when we drowsily get out of the mini-van in Ban Tha Klang. Mahouts, each with a chequered piece of cloth around his head, are standing shivering near small fires as it's still cold. Roosters are crowing, dogs are barking, but there is no line of monks, and no prime minister. Lee goes to investigate. The starting time appears to have been moved to nine o'clock, and the prime minister has turned into some general who will come later.

We take a peek at the festival grounds, a huge field with stands on two sides. Over a stage is a sign: 'The elephants will return to their habitat of old, Surin'. On the field are rows of tables covered with sugar cane, pineapple, and bananas—an elephant buffet. We cross a stubbled field, circumventing the guards. They look frightful with their hats and sunglasses, but I do believe Lee enjoys acting the anarchist. Sometimes he says, 'We are spies!' with a twinkle in his eye, and today he has brought the '*Bring the elephant home*' banner under his jacket with a mysterious look on his face, ready to unfold it at the right moment.

Trucks loaded with sugar cane and banana trees drive to and fro. Elephants are everywhere. Little ones like Taeng-kwa, 'Cucumber', recently taken from his mother to be trained. There is a large elephant with a missing rear foot. Stepped on a landmine, like Malai Thong. Most of the mahouts and their families are shabby and skinny. We do a brief survey. What do they think of the mahout salary? 'It is a good thing,' a darkly tanned, tawny old man says, 'if it doesn't stop after a month. That remains to be seen. In Bangkok I can make more money, but it's a very demanding life.' 'Not bad,' another mahout says, 'but where will we get food for the elephants? There is plenty today, but tomorrow? Now we have support from the government, but tomorrow?'

We meet an old friend: Wichian, the flirty mahout. He didn't register for the mahout salary. He doesn't trust it, he says, it will mainly benefit the rich elephant traders. Businessmen, who own one or two hundred elephants. When the government honours their claims, they will take the lion's share of the budget. He doesn't think eight thousand baht is enough. A street elephant is accompanied by at least three mahouts, their families have to eat, and so do the elephants. When one has to meet all kinds of government demands for that amount of money, he would rather go without.

I do some math. At the Elephant Nature Park a mahout gets 4,500 baht a month, about 95 euros. The additional feeding for an elephant costs 6,000 baht a month. A total of 10,500 baht, more than the 8,000 the government is offering the mahouts to stay home. At the very least it means that elephant food has to be planted around the villages, so that it doesn't have to be bought.

At nine o'clock, the grounds and the stands start to fill up. There're a lot of press cameras around, so apparently the mahout salary is a newsworthy subject. Near the entrance, there's some commotion, has the general arrived? I plunge into the crowd, camera at the ready, and, as a white person, immediately get a clear path. Try that in Holland as a brown person. At the centre of the anthill, I find a much better spectacle than a general: the old heroes of Ban Tha Klang, the legendary shamans, catchers of wild elephants. No longer lithe, and with big spectacles wobbling in front of nearsighted eyes, but their proud demeanour still speaks of the toughness of their younger days. Their tattooed old men's bodies are shrouded in ceremonial Khmer clothing, silk trousers, beautifully woven shawls in earth colours. Some are sporting the buffalo horns they would sound during the hunt to warn each other.

I recognise Mr. Boonma. He is standing with his chest out, his gaze on the distant horizons where he used to catch elephants. When he sees me, he smiles broadly, and then falls back into his noble pose. The group of old heroes walks to an altar surrounded with flowers. On it is the sacred buffalo hide rope. They kneel in front of it and burn incense. Then the solemn part of the programme is over and modern needs can be satisfied: photo opportunity! The elderly men line up and everyone can photograph them or have their picture taken with them. The best image occurs when a group of police officers positions itself in front of the shamans. Their helmets and sunglasses project a completely different kind of authority from that of the old men behind them.

At ten thirty, the general strides onto the grounds, followed by fifty men and one woman. He proceeds towards the stage, and while the elephants are waiting on the other side of the buffet, an endless succession of speeches follows. Even Lee loses interest. Suddenly he pulls out our banner. 'Camera standby!' On top of the stands we unfold our *'Bring the elephant home'* banner in Thai and in English, for all the cameras to see, with the hope of making the nine o'clock news. Lee grins with satisfaction. Then, finally, at the end of the morning, the elephants get to eat. There is no stampede, as one might expect. Like ladies and gentlemen of standing the giants stroll over to the tables, and in their own, slow way they eat with relish. Even though, I must say, I have never seen gentlemen or ladies of standing squeeze out a pineapple into their mouth in one go, then casually sling the remaining pulp thirty feet behind them.

The whole thing is over early in the afternoon. We take a walk through Ban Tha Klang. Hey, a sign: 'Home Stay Mahout Programme.' The building is closed of course, as the elephants and their mahouts aren't at home today. In the courtyard, a comprehensive text is fixed to a wall. It says that seventy percent of the baby elephants working in tourism come from the wild. Frequently, the mothers are killed in the hunt for the young animals. The programme wants to put a stop to this, as well as to illegal logging and begging with elephants. The ways to do this are mentioned as well: ecotourism in the villages, education for mahouts, making tourists familiar with Thai culture and with the lives of the mahouts, and reforestation around the villages.

That sounds good. Why have I never heard about this? I knew about attempts to find a real solution for the Surin elephants, once in 2003. Back then the ban on street elephants came into effect, and seventy mahouts and their animals simultaneously returned to Surin, where there was no food at that time. The desperate mahouts decided to take action and organised a protest march to Bangkok, together with their elephants. The government budgeted a large amount of money to bring them to a nature reserve. The idea was to turn the elephants and the mahouts into park rangers. But once there, they were left to their own device. There was no supervision, no organisation. Wild stories were told about this failure. The mahouts supposedly couldn't handle life in the forest, were afraid of forest spirits, their foot soles were too tender, and they always wanted to be in charge. The domesticated elephants supposedly came into conflict with the wild ones, or the domesticated ones couldn't take all that jungle anymore. They should take a look at Lilly when she runs into the forest at Elephant Haven. Of all those so-called reasons, that one, I think, is the most far-fetched of all.

At the bottom of the text of the Home Stay Mahout Programme, I read that one can be a volunteer, with some mahout training included. There is a phone number. It is music to my ears. I call right away, and get Mr. Arnon, the manager, on the phone. 'Ban Tha Klang? No, I'm sorry, we have moved to Pattaya. Come to Pattaya to be a volunteer!' Apparently, the project in Ban Tha Klang has failed. Problems with the village chief, Mr. Arnon says. He was well disposed towards the project and he was involved, but had a different perspective. Instead of bamboo huts for the guests, luxury chalets sprung up, and what's more, suddenly an elephant show was included in the programme. There were problems with the mahouts as well. They didn't feel like working and started their days with whiskey.

But why didn't the mahouts want to work? A job in the project would seem much better than begging in Bangkok. For now those are questions without answers. The music in my ears has gone a little off key. But when Si-nuan and Dok-ngeon are safely at the Park, I will go and take a look in Pattaya.

On the road back, I dream for a while that I'm home in Holland. My return ticket is missing. Desperately, I turn closets and bags inside out. When I wake up because of the cold—air-conditioning is a disaster, I always have the sniffles after long car trips—I realise I want to stay in Thailand for a good while. I long for the time when the weight will be off my shoulders, and I can take things on at my own pace.

Once back at the camp, I fall in love with a puppy that is wandering motherless around the hall. It's no more than two months old, the colour of café au lait, two floppy ears, one of them pointing down. I give him dog food and take him on my lap. When I stop petting him, he starts whining and shaking. After five minutes, I already want to keep him with me forever. Get real, Antoinette, you cannot keep a dog out here. But what if I take him to the Park? Yeah right, they already have thirty dogs. But can't Hanna take him back to Holland? Ever heard of quarantine and expensive vaccinations? And how are you going to take care of a dog considering you're hardly ever at home? Mmmm. That night he sleeps in a basket close to me. But outside, because he is riddled with fleas. At night he scratches my tent. I call him Pa Kaeo, after the temple.

9

Reinforcements

MONDAY, MOVING DAY. For the third time, Si-nuan has broken down the tree she was tethered to during night. Lee promises the monks to send fifty seedlings of *krissana*, a tree with fragrant blossoms that is popular in temple compounds.

Together with Nong, Oey, and Yut, we break camp and load the mini-van. Nachon drives the truck to a spot where the elephants can step up into it easily. Pa Kaeo is watching all the activity with a sad look. Am I left alone again? Doctor Nit looks at me. '*Pa Kaeo pai Chiang Mai?*' Is Pa Kaeo coming to Chiang Mai with us? Lee is signalling that we really have to get going. Si-nuan and Dokngeon smoothly get on the truck, which is filled with fruit. The caravan takes off. Lee and I take Doctor Nit's car to go and thank the construction company who let us use its land for the elephants to graze on. Pa Kaeo is walking all alone around the empty space left by our camp. 'Lee . . .' I say hesitantly when we drive away from the construction company, 'I keep thinking of Pa Kaeo. I think it's so sad that we left him behind.' 'Do you want to take him on our trip?' 'Yes. Life at the Elephant Nature Park might be better for him than it is here.' Lee thinks about it for a while. Then he says: 'Okay, we'll pick him up. Pa Kaeo could always live with my father, he loves dogs.' I feel like I'm seven years old again, when my father gave me permission to buy a dog after endless begging. We race back to the temple, where Pa Kaeo is still wandering around on his own. I pick him up and jump in the car. Pa Kaeo is coming on our trip! Doctor Nit magically finds a soft cloth and puppy food. I still have to figure out his destination, but I am so happy with his company. Lopburi is only about seventy miles from Ayutthaya, so the trip only takes two hours, and my dog's behaviour is exemplary. It's almost as if he has separation anxiety, since he only sleeps when he is in my lap. How did he ever get house-trained?

Our next campsite is three miles outside Lopburi, between rice fields. It's called Wat Mongkhon Prasit, and it's a collection of real Thai temple buildings with frills, gold, and mirror mosaics that sparkle with every ray of light, especially at night. It's too bad the temple is near a motorway, where traffic roars by from as early as six o'clock in the morning. Behind the prayer hall are dozens of miniature *chedi*, monuments commemorating deceased monks and nuns. In the centre of the grounds is a pond with tortoises and carps, while surrounding it are the dwellings of the monks and nuns. They are really tiny, no more than eleven square yards I suppose, but I'd choose one of these any day over a hundred square yards in an Amsterdam suburb. The nuns welcome us and pet Pa Kaeo, who I can't let go of. 'Did you bring him along from Ayutthaya? Leave him here, we'll take good care of him.' No way, he is coming with us, at least as far as Chiang Mai.

I would have liked to put up the tents near the elephants, outside the temple walls. In Ayutthaya I have spent too little time with Si-nuan and Dok-ngeon, I miss their big, grey presence and their sounds. But the nuns advise against it, as does Duang. 'Far too many mosquitoes out there,' he says. We compromise; our tents underneath the trees near the prayer hall, the elephants in the field during the day, and with us at night. The drivers and the cooking team set up the kitchen and their own tents indoors, inside one of the temple buildings. City slickers! But their spot does become the warm, lively centre of the camp; it's where we are when we are 'home'. Yut and Nong's jokes, Oey and Nachon's quiet reliability, and little Ford scurrying around; the part English, part Thai language we are developing, all of it is colouring camp life. Not to mention the aromas coming from the kitchen. Today it's Nachon's birthday, we celebrate it with cake. While we are digging into it, Lee comes running in: 'I *checkbin* with Nong!' But Nong doesn't have time for accounting, she is in a fight with Hanna about how to cut up an onion. 'No good! Taohu, I cooking!' 'I cooking *di mak*, very good!' says Hanna. The only one not welcome in the kitchen is Pa Keao. Time for him to have a bath, I decide. My buckets of water are not met with gratitude. After the washing, Doctor Nit comes over with flea powder, a flea injection, a vitamin injection, and worm pills. With two ears down, Pa Kaeo skulks into the kitchen. Yut shakes his head, as a dog in a Thai kitchen is unheard of. But he can stay.

Doctor Nit, Lee, and I take off to the animal office in the city to arrange for the permits. No problem, quite the contrary in fact. When Lee explains our goal, the eyes of the official in charge grow round with amazement, and finally he comes towards me with open arms, shakes my hand warmly, and says: 'Very good, wonderful!' These expressions of support still surprise me after the endless worries about permits.

I send out a stack of press releases from an Internet cafe, hoping for some media attention. When we go back into town later to stock up on supplies, we end up at the home of an old lady who is taking care of seventy street dogs. So Thailand has them as well, people collecting hordes of animals. I do understand, of course, after all I have just recently acquired two little cows, two large elephants, and a temple puppy. But this woman is living in a miserable slum. Her dwelling and yard cap everything. Some dogs are on chains, others walk around freely. Some growl fearsomely. They live among a vast mountain of half decayed rubbish. The woman is not very popular with the neighbours. There are many drug addicts in the neighbourhood, and next to the woman lives a drug dealer. The dogs and the addicts fight each other at night, and the woman says some of her dogs have been poisoned. We give her some money. She will use it to buy new tires for her cart, she says. She uses it to sell things on the street and collect new stuff. We promise to come back with medicines for the dogs. She cries.

***

Cats and dogs are everywhere in Wat Mongkhon Prasit as well. On the morning of our first animal clinic, they are brought in by the nuns with wheel barrows, and Doctor Nit rolls up her sleeves. Later Lee and I go to find the headman of the neighbouring village. Along the way, I notice an old woman with a dark red mouth from chewing betel nut, and stripped to the waist, sitting in front of a shop. I stare in total amazement, since I thought Asian women always covered their breasts. 'Oh no,' Lee says, 'a hundred years ago all old women would dress like this.'

We meet village chief Vichai Sumetratanasri at his home. A big man, radiating authority. He turns out to be a retired military man. Nowadays he does services for the village for a low salary, just like his father and grandfather before him. The porch in front of the house serves as an office. There is a desk with a typewriter, with a pillow on top serving as a cover to keep out the dust. Behind it is an aquarium, without fish, but with a framed certificate, and a spray can against insects. There's also a flaking whiteboard with notes on it, partially hidden by a flowery umbrella. On the wall hang a picture of Mickey

Mouse, a calendar with a portrait of the King, and a calendar with a nude lady, her breasts covered up with something that looks like a by-law. Mr. Vichai sits with a benevolent gaze behind a table bearing a huge sound system, an important tool, as we are to find out in the coming week.

He has received word about our coming from the animal office, and we can count on his co-operation. A team from a Lopburi cable-TV station might come if we can fork out ten euros 'for gas and stuff'. A school programme is a possibility, as they have one large school for the children of three villages. Tomorrow morning, we can set up the animal clinic at the village square. Mr. Vichai picks up his cell phone and within fifteen minutes our entire week's schedule is fixed. In the meantime, I quietly roll back and forth in the bamboo rocking chair that is part of the office furnishings as well. I wouldn't mind sitting here when I'm old—topless, and with a red betel nut stained mouth.

Mr. Vichai takes us to the regional headquarters of the six villages, including his. We find ourselves in an entirely different kind of office, with air-conditioning, shiny tiles, and a secretary who brings cups of coffee, while bowing profusely. The assembled dignitaries are as enthusiastic as Mr. Vichai. After Lee has explained our mission, their leader grabs my hand and announces: 'Excellent lady! We are Thai, we can do only little to solve the elephant problem. Foreigners can do so much. You get back beautiful life from the gods.'

The mobile animal clinic is becoming an important part of our programme. It is a good way to get people to come to us, and to introduce the *Bring the elephant home* project. Besides, we can contribute to the well-being of the animals and the people. In Mr. Vichai's village, the animal clinic is a success as well. After we've set up our tables in the village square, Mr. Vichai announces the glad tidings of our arrival over his sound system. His voice fills every nook and cranny of the village for at least fifteen minutes, while he talks about the project, encourages people to come and visit our elephants, and announces the free pet treatments. It doesn't take long for the first dog and owner to appear. 'We have a case!' Lee calls out with enthusiasm: after that we are swamped. A muzzled Doberman with a scared-looking owner, a Chihuahua in a blue sweater, a bulldog in a bee-outfit, a spotted mongrel with a tortured look, a rickety monk with an even more rickety Pomeranian, a cardboard box with five kittens, and a military man with eight dogs he saved from certain death by taking care of them when his officers wanted to have them put down because of troop movements. Long waiting rows form, but chairs are brought in, and the occasion turns into a cheerful village event with coffee, soft drinks, and cake supplied by the headman's secretary. An ice-cream truck arrives, and even the dignitaries of the regional head office come and take a look. We have put up our large banner and the large posters with elephant pictures. Every visitor is handed one of our leaflets. Somebody brings in a load of free sugar cane for the elephants. That same night, the owner of the field where Si-nuan and Dok-ngeon are grazing brings a pile of banana trees. We're a big hit in Lopburi.

Mr. Vichai has adopted us whole-heartedly. He and his sound system accompany us at every activity this week, and in the evening he joins us for dinner. 'We have managed to win over some important people,' Lee says.

Meanwhile, our team has expanded again. Duang's wife has joined us. We remember Yan Madee from Surin, a happy, robust woman who immediately puts her shoulder to the wheel. She helps with the cooking and cleaning, and travels with us to the Elephant Nature Park.

By now, Pa Kaeo's basket is in my tent. But he is not satisfied with that anymore, now he wants to be next to me on my pillow. When I push him away, he whimpers as if a great injustice has been done him. All right, outside you go Pa Kaeo. Loud protesting. First he tries to dig and then chew his way in; finally he manages to get his nose between a zipper and wriggles inside. I get the giggles, and he gets what he wants.

It is nice to have the elephants close by at night. I hear their breathing and their grinding teeth. When I crawl out of my tent in the middle of the night, I even see them lying asleep in the moonlight. A sight to remember.

***

Si-nuan and Dok-ngeon are in the Promised Land, and eat till their bellies bulge. They can drink from the irrigation canals of the surrounding rice fields. Strangely enough though, they don't bathe. Every now and then they hose themselves down, but they don't go in the water. I spend an afternoon with them. Duang and Narong are the mahouts of the day.

Since the field is next to the water, there are a lot of mosquitoes, biting flies, and dragonflies. Duang uses his flip-flop to chase them away from the elephants. 'Look,' he says as he points out a small bloodstain behind Si-nuan's ear, 'An elephant even bleeds from an insect bite.' The proverbial thick-skinned insensitivity of an elephant is a fairy-tale, like their stamping. Their skin is thick, in some places almost two inches, but delicate as well. That is a reason why an elephant protects himself from insects with water and dust baths.

Narong, twenty-five, small and sturdy, comes from a village near Chiang Mai. A large cross is tattooed on his chest. Like all his Karen village, he was raised a Christian. He has worked with elephants from the age of ten. 'My family has always kept elephants. Today we have two, working in a trekking camp. All my brothers and sisters are mahouts.' Does he ever talk to them about the different approach of the Park? 'They use the hooked goad, but mainly to steer the elephant in the right direction. The Park is good to the animals, it is a new way to deal with them, and you can learn a lot there. But honestly, I sometimes think the situation is unsafe. When an elephant is restless and doesn't want to listen, you often can't handle him without a goad. This is difficult for me, especially when there are children and tourists nearby. Elephants and people are not the same. They eat grass, we eat rice.'

If he really had a choice, he would go back to school. 'I would like to have a good education. But as long as that is not possible, I will work with elephants. At the Park, for now, though in the long run perhaps somewhere else. The Park doesn't pay as much as working with tourists. But going elsewhere doesn't mean I will treat the elephants differently.'

A point in the Park's favour, he says, is the contact with the volunteers. 'It is good for my English, and there are always pretty girls. It is too bad they always leave again. I make a lot of new friends, but then later miss them. You will stay, won't you?' He shows me his address book with all his foreign girls.

The owner of the field comes by with an axe. We can chop down some banana trees a little down the road. I jump between Si-nuan and Narong to go to the banana field, and accidentally step over Narong's hat. That's a mortal sin in Thailand. The head, and everything that belongs to it, is sacred and you can't touch it or point at it. And touching it with your feet is even worse, feet are way down on the ladder. Narong explodes. 'You've been in Thailand so many times, and still don't respect our culture!' Shaken, I apologise. Narong grabs his hat and walks away, muttering. Fortunately, Duang still wants to talk to me.

'The elephants in Chiang Mai are there for tourism,' he says, 'while in Surin we preserve the tradition of the elephant as a symbol of Thailand. The annual festival is a national event, everybody prepares for it.' But aren't most Surin elephants street elephants these days? 'That's true. The work with tourists has become the main source of income for mahout families in Surin as well. Most of them also grow rice, but if you want your children to go to school, you have to make more money. Fifty or a hundred baht for a ride, that's adding up nicely. Besides, nowadays the elephants get more food in the city than they do at home.'

Duang is now getting into his stride. So far I have known him as a silent force, the mahout who is the first one up and the last to go to sleep. As he goes on talking about his life as a mahout, he becomes passionate. 'The government wants to buy elephants and release them into the wild. That is not going to work. They will walk back to the rice fields, back to the people. The Elephant Nature Park might be a good project, but it will take a long time before the government realises it.'

He isn't pleased with the mahout salary. 'They pay eight thousand baht, that is not enough for a family, when you have to take care of an elephant as well. How can you get by if you don't have land to grow food on? There is not enough land.'

Duang's family has always kept elephants. 'They used to be caught in the forest, now we buy them. They are a big part of our lives. You feed them and you bring them up. Fourteen years ago, when I saw how much money others could make with them, I took an elephant into the city for the first time. It provides a stable income. I was able to send my children to school, and buy fertiliser for the rice. But now we are kicked out everywhere and we are fined all the time. You can only get into Bangkok if you pay nine hundred baht. Sometimes I'm away from home two or three months at a stretch. I have had enough. Our elephants have become a problem, a burden.'

A different kind of work with elephants is not an option. 'Some businessmen and politicians own many elephants and lend or hire them out to mahouts to go and beg. But when there is a lot of money to be made, at festivals, for example, they put it in their own pockets. There are also elephant camps with activities for tourists, and there you get a salary of four thousand baht. But in the high season, with money pouring in, the mahouts still get four thousand baht. I prefer to do the banana thing in the city, at least you are your own boss.'

The next day Duang's son calls. The government has announced that they will give every family that stays home with its elephant a salary of eight thousand baht, and a piece of land. Duang's son has signed up for it.

***

Pa Kaeo is bigger every day. He has gnawed a hole in Doctor Nit's tent, and has made friends with three white puppies hanging about the temple grounds of Mongkhon Prasit. Doctor Nit, for her part, has made friends with one of the three puppies, and it looks like our menagerie is about to expand again.

In the evening, the nuns come to feed the elephants bananas, and they visit us in our kitchen more and more frequently. They are curious about us, and we about them. Despite the language problems, we have long conversations. 'Khit thueng,' Sister Mae Si says, while taking pictures of the elephants and of us with her cell phone. *Khit thueng*, we don't know that word. Mae Si searches her English vocabulary for a word that comes close. 'I love you!' she suddenly says triumphantly. '*Khit thueng* means missing,' Lee says later on. 'She means that she will think of us after we have left.' Mae Si invites me into her hut. As tiny as it is, I still don't know where to look first. The only pieces of furniture are a bed, a little table, decorated as an altar, and a low work bench. The altar is covered with portraits. I see monks, the queen-mother, and an old lady, Mae Si's own mother. Surrounding them are religious items, statues, candle holders, garlands, and a digital alarm clock. The work bench is buried under knick-knacks, little pots, bottles, notes, a glass with pens in it, a table lamp with a low-energy light bulb, and two boxes of paper tissues. Along the walls and underneath the bed are other boxes and baskets. A whole life concentrated into a few square feet. Nevertheless, the room is spotlessly tidy.

We communicate with a lot of gestures. Mae Si used to be a nurse in Chiang Mai though now she loves life in the monastery. She gives me an amulet with the image of a monk. 'He lives in the woods,' she says, 'a very strict monk. Many people visit him. When he asks for money to build a temple, it is raised within a month.' She asks if I have seen the ancient buildings of Lopburi yet. The palace of King Narai is something I have to go and see.

I walk back to the kitchen past the pond with the tortoises and carps. Lee is scrubbing toilets. He doesn't just pray at every temple he comes across, he doesn't just make offerings in every alms bowl, he scrubs toilets too. Lee can look forward to a beautiful next life.

King Narai lived in the seventeenth century. Ayutthaya was his official seat of government, but he built a palace in Lopburi where he spent three quarters of the year. Most of the palace buildings have no roofs anymore, and only the foundations remain of others, but the whole picture is still beautiful. Just as in the historical park at Ayutthaya, you can stroll through the past at your leisure. You enter at a measured pace through one of the entrance gates in the huge wall surrounding the grounds—pace is the only correct word. The gate is more than wide and high enough for the elephants that Narai, as all Thai kings, kept in his stables. You automatically feel important when you pass through the thick walls, high above your head the gate roof with gable ends on four sides are covered with shiny, glazed roof tiles and decorated with stucco lotus flowers. The same floral shape is repeated in the many niches, evenly spaced in the gate building and meant to hold lanterns. Similar recesses are built into the walls that surround the middle and inner courts of the palace grounds. Two thousand in all, I read in the booklet I buy at the entrance. The light from two thousand lanterns flickering on the centuries old wall: how I would love to see that.

The walls were built under the supervision of an Italian priest. King Narai maintained good relationships with other countries. The remnants of the waterworks, constructed by French and Italian engineers also testify to this, as does the building where the envoys of the French Sun King were received. There are windows of Thai and French design right above one another. Indeed, historical sources tell us that because of Narai's foreigner-friendly policies, a coup was being hatched against him in the palace monastery.

Not much is left of the elephant halls in the middle court. In an attempt to compensate for this, the art of topiary has been employed—bushes artfully trimmed into elephant shapes. Si-nuan and Dok-ngeon would make a nice picture against the weather-beaten walls with the niches. But given the temptation of the large trees that dot the grounds, they had better stay in their field.

I also visit Phra Prang Sam Yot, near the train station. It consists of three pagodas in a row in the by now familiar corncob style. They are largely intact. Inside, between ancient stones in all shades of brown and grey, it is cool. Thai youngsters are praying and lighting incense sticks before a Buddha statue. Outside is the realm of the monkeys. They are macaques, a small kind of monkey with huge ears, black tufts, and surprised-looking eyes in crumpled little faces. The ticket-salesman urges me to keep my bag firmly closed, and hands me a stick. A little exaggerated, I think, until I spot a screaming Japanese tourist struggling with a monkey with his paws clamped in her hair. The animals are very taken with the tourists, and the tourists with them in return. I don't see the 'fat temple monkeys' the French journalist in Ayutthaya told me about, though. A little later, in the city, I do see a monkey snatching a box of milk cartons from a lorry and tossing it down onto the street, after which he opens a carton with ease and pours the contents into his mouth. I buy a bag of bread rolls. Suddenly, a sizeable macaque is standing in front of me, his eyes fixed on the rolls. He jumps at me, as I throw the bag away with a scream. The monkey snatches it up, sits down on a pillar, pulls out a roll, throws me a defiant look and starts eating at his leisure. His brother, a little further down the road, is drinking a super-sized coke.

In the end I get to see the fat temple monkeys. In the trees surrounding a temple, a monkey climbing circuit has been built with nets, rope ladders, and swings. Drinking bowls are everywhere, and scattered among them are mounds of food. There is a tiny old lady who has dedicated her life to taking care of the temple monkeys. She brings in the food in a wheel barrow, after that she sits on a bench, contentedly watching. When I leave the temple, I see a gang of street monkeys hanging out on a roundabout. The cars wait for the group to move on. The Lopburi animal office must have a heavy work load.

At a stand, I buy *khao tom mat* for forty euro cents. Sticky rice with pieces of banana, wrapped in banana leaves, grilled on charcoal. At a neighbouring stand, a woman is making *khanom khrok*. In every hole of a pancake griddle she puts a little butter, then some sweet coconut milk. All the holes are carefully filled with dough, after which the griddle is put on the charcoal fire. Eating on the street is great in Thailand. You can get good food everywhere and at every time of day or night. The preparation is an art form in itself.

I walk back to Wat Mongkhon Prasit through the rice fields. Pa Kaeo greets me happily. Everybody goes to bed around nine o'clock, since tomorrow we are setting off with the elephants very early. While I upload my photographs onto the laptop and start recharging the batteries, I hear Narong in the shower singing a song I know but can't quite place. When I sing along in Dutch, I recognise it: Silent night, holy night.

***

Mr. Vichai has arranged for us to hold the elephant programme at the Thanon Kae primary school, and on Children's Day to boot. On this day, parents come to school to see if their children are doing their best. But unlike our dreaded parent-teacher conferences, this is a festive happening with snacks and ice-cream, song and dance. Of course, the day will start with monks who, with their alms bowls, allow us to make offerings of food to earn some spiritual welfare. They always do this at daybreak, and so we are on the road even before dawn. It is about a mile to the village. It is obvious that Si-nuan and Dok-ngeon are street elephants, as cool as a cucumber among the speeding traffic. I'm not, I am utterly miserable, and walk in the middle of the street to keep the cars away from the elephants, thereby actually worsening the situation. How could I ever have thought we could quietly walk through Thailand? Poor elephants, I promised them they would never have to walk on the streets again. Just how far is it to this school? Lee disappears into a field to try to find a short-cut, but returns without having accomplished his mission. Barbed wire everywhere. 'This is what happened to the British couple in 2003,' he says. 'All the way from Ayutthaya to Nakhon Sawan, mostly in the verge or on the street.' Again I think, why didn't I know of this? I wouldn't have lasted a day as it feels terribly wrong, so I am happy our walk was finally cancelled.

In the village, a different kind of danger looms. Si-nuan grabs every branch she can reach, even the chief of police's wife's carefully tended bougainvillaea. Duang proves himself the experienced street mahout that he is. He watches the road's surface, kicks glass out of the way, and leads the elephants past the drain covers that might give way. Wiset walks next to Dok-ngeon, Narong sits on Si-nuan, and enters the village as if he were Julius Caesar. Is it so hard to imagine why little boys revere mahouts? Who would want to be a bus driver when you can steer an elephant? Even though the magic of elephants may be somewhat diminished, I do still see awe, everywhere we go.

On the school grounds, the animals find a spot reserved for them at the edge of a sports field in the shade of some trees. Lee has arranged for an enclosure to be set up, and a truckload of banana tree trunks delivered. The children crowd round the elephants, just like they did in Ayutthaya, and breathlessly watch Si-nuan splitting a banana tree trunk across her leg. Dok-ngeon's top act is spreading her hind legs to drop several substantial turds.

Many children are dressed in traditional garb. Some, even the boys, wear make-up. Lipstick, blusher, eye shadow, the entire paint box. A woman teacher brings a sign that says 'Welcome at the Thanon Kae School Si-nuan, Dok-ngeon and *Bring the elephant home*,' in a funny computer font that we use in Holland quite often as well. In some ways the world has become a large village.

At eight forty-five, the monks arrive. Fifteen of them, the youngest is about thirty, the eldest almost in the next life. He is in a wheelchair, his orange robes have turned a pale yellow from all the washing, and he doesn't wear shoes. 'Very strict!' Lee whispers. He is in awe of the monk. 'He made sure that money was gathered to establish this school. Education is very important to him.' Everyone kneels, parents, children, teachers, and all of us. The elderly monk starts a long chant of blessing. The sun scorches our heads. When it's over, the monks come by with their alms bowls. In earlier days, everyone grew rice and gave some of it to the temple, today people buy prepacked buckets of food stuffs. The orange cellophane around them conveys their purpose. Lee has advised us to make up packages containing fruit juice, soy milk, tea, and a package of noodle soup, spicy flavour. During the chanting, I had already wondered about how the monks could get all this food into their begging bowls, but as usual there is a practical Thai solution. Behind every monk is someone with a big bag into which the full begging bowls are emptied. Perishables that the monks don't eat themselves, will be laid out in the temple public hall. People in need can come and get them.

Led by the teaching staff, parents and children move off to an open-sided pavilion behind the school where the festivities will be held. We'll be performing at the end. Everywhere children are drawing and colouring elephants. Across the sports field, the mini-van lurches towards us, carrying Yut, Nong, Nachon, Oey, baby Ford, and our campaign materials.

We open the animal clinic, together with doctors from the animal office this time. In co-operation with *Bring the elephant home,* they neuter and spay dogs and cats. The surgery has been set up on the basketball field, close to the trees where Si-nuan and Dok-ngeon are. I see the blades and hope they won't really do it here in the open air. But before I can even blink, three dogs lay unconscious on the table. A slight feeling of unreality comes over me. Three hundred and fifty children with their parents, two elephants in a sports field, our entire team in red T-shirts, a growing pile of dog and cat balls on the surgical table, Mr. Vichai, who is acting as ringmaster of this circus with his sound system, the local dignitaries, and yes, there is ITV's television camera. How could I ever have set these wheels in motion?

The headmaster invites us to the pavilion to watch. The children are performing songs and dances with their classes, traditional style with a touch of MTV. The music is playing at war strength, and is controlled through a laptop by a teacher who slightly resembles our Queen Beatrix. At the end of the programme, a thundering techno beat erupts from the speakers. 'Queen Beatrix'

Fig 43. School children visit Dok-ngeon and Si-nuan in our Sukhothai camping ground

Fig 44. Si-nuan leaves primary school in Sukhothai

Fig 45. Duang

Fig 46. Chaotic arrival in the Elephant Nature Park

Fig 47. Si-nuan and Dok-ngeon freshen up

Fig 48. Lee, happy that his 'daughters' are home (photo: Hanna Jongepier)

Fig 49. Lilly and her mahout Bochu

Fig 50. Si-nuan and Lilly crash into each other

Fig 51. Hope and his mahout Duvet

Fig 52. The new family, left to right: Mae Tokoh, Dok-ngeon, Pupia, Si-nuan, and Malai Thong

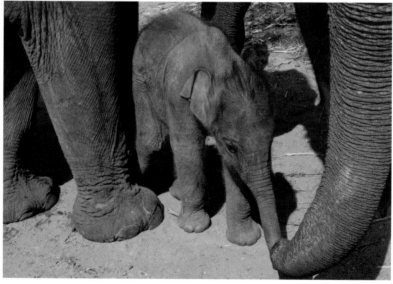

Fig 53. Pupia sniffs out Si-nuan

Fig 54. Antoinette and Pupia

Fig 55. Si-nuan and Antoinette

Fig 56. Happy ending

nervously looks at the stage behind her. A boy of about fourteen years of age jumps onto the stage in sexy shorts, a yellow blouse, and with painted lips and nails. He does a pole dancing act without the pole, while the crowd cheers tumultuously. You see them everywhere in Thailand, lady boys, boys in all stages of girlhood. It is accepted, although not respected and certainly not talked about publicly. 'Queen Beatrix' is having a hard time, she messes with the laptop until the music falls apart, and the enthusiasm of the audience diminishes audibly. The boy bravely finishes his act, but the spirit has gone.

Then the headmaster announces us and we get off to a good start with the *Chang* song. Because the parents want to go home early in the afternoon, we shorten the programme. Songs, elephant quiz, letter game, it runs like clockwork with Lee's cheerful presentation. The drawings the children have made today and during the past few days at school are wonderful once more. Duang, Narong, and Wiset choose the winning artists, and strangely it is the Disney-like elephants that win their approval.

When we pack up, we keep tripping over the many dogs that, anaesthetised and with bloody behinds, are strewn across the sports field, waiting for their owners to come and pick them up. We have lunch with the people from the animal office and they take us to their headquarters, to take care of the paperwork for the elephant transport to Sukhothai. At the office, everybody is talking about *Bring the elephant home*. Those who had to stay behind jealously ask the neutering team what it was like. When Lee takes out the newspaper article with my picture in it, everybody gathers around. Is it really her? Cell phones appear, photographs and films are made. The chief of the provincial animal office comes in and greets us kindly. He has just been complimented by his colleagues in Bangkok. 'I called them to ask for advice about how to deal with you. Now they are proud about us working together so well, and they hope you will work together with animal offices on other projects.'

'That was very extraordinary,' Lee says later on. 'The government wants to co-operate with us!' In the evening, I call Pa Kaeo. Drowsily he walks a few feet, then sits down until I pick him up. He is turning into a Dutch dog. In the tent we fight over the pillow again, he wins. I wake up at night, because he is sniffing around in my ear. I hear snoring, who is that? It can't be Lee, far too loud. It's Si-nuan. A deep, peaceful sound rumbles through her enormous forehead.

10

Destinations

THE TENTS ARE down as early as six o'clock, so at a quarter past seven Si-nuan and Dok-ngeon obediently step into the truck, while the nuns are waving goodbye. We drive north along the irrigation canals. We have gained another team member; Doctor Nit has brought along a white puppy. Just like Pa Kaeo, she is named after her temple of origin, Mongkhon. I get into the cabin of the truck with Nachon and Lee. You can feel the truck shaking when one of the elephants in the back stirs as she adjusts her stance. 'Just keep steering. Drive calmly, brake slowly,' Nachon says, never a man of many words. After fifteen minutes, the roof of the cabin is suddenly bombarded. What's up? Si-nuan has found the bags of food in the luggage compartment at the back of the cabin. She has opened one, and now it is raining cucumbers.

Along the roadside, we see booths with lotus fruit, and large garden cen-tres and construction supermarkets. As soon as the sun is fully up, Lee, always edgy on the road, is using a magnifying glass to study the map of Thailand on which the road from Lopburi to Sukhothai is an almost perfect straight line. When he has checked it top to bottom three times, he takes his catapult out of his bag and says with his James Bond look: 'My gun!' His apprehen-sion is probably provoked by the memory of the trip with the British couple in 2003; suddenly he starts to talk about it. 'The route was drawn out on the map every day, but some of the roads marked on the map didn't even exist. For example, we would suddenly find ourselves on a river bank and have to go back ten miles. Usually we walked along the roads. We had to pay bribes all the time, and I had to show my identification papers everywhere.' Talk of the devil: right at that moment we have to stop for a 'veterinary inspection' office. A pink building, with two cows in front of it. Lee grabs his papers and disappears inside. He returns after just a few minutes, with a big smile. No, the permit nightmare is definitely over.

Duang and Wiset keep Si-nuan and Dok-ngeon company in the back of the truck. Duang keeps a close eye on the animals and comforts them. Almost sixty—and he thinks little of sitting for several hundred miles on a pole wedged crosswise in the truck at elephant chest height. Due to stress, the elephants have emptied their bowels and bladders, so it is like a pig-sty back there. But things could be worse, as we soon see at a petrol station. The cargo hold of a truck has been so heavily loaded with buffaloes that the horns stick out through the slats. Steel wires through their noses bind them fast to bars above them. There is no tailboard at the back but a net, bulging with a buffalo that was the last to be crammed in. It has its eyes closed, as if to escape this buffalo hell by meditating. The people of the petrol station bring sugar cane and bread for the elephants. Lee gives an inspired speech about *Bring the elephant home* to the truckers at the soda dispenser. 'You are a fine ambassador,' I say. 'That is the concept of my job,' he says.

By late in the afternoon, we reach Sukhothai, 'Dawn of Happiness'. It is the capital of a province that is hilly in the north, and a river plain for the remainder, an important agricultural area. Wat Ban Na is on a five mile long road between the old and the new Sukhothai. The temple grounds are spacious with lots of buildings scattered around. We pitch camp next to the monks' dwellings, underneath a group of tall, straight teak trees. 'Planted in love for nature,' a small sign proclaims. We immediately clean out two toilets, one gent's, one lady's, while the mahouts take Si-nuan and Dok-ngeon across the street to fields where rice has already been harvested. The elephants head straight for a lonely tree, and scrunch scrunch, crack crack, the lower half of the foliage is gone. Duang walks into the fields and comes back satisfied. A bit further on there is plenty of grass and water. Then we take the mini-van to new Sukhothai to buy bananas, and spot a small street elephant on the way back. Here, too, they're clearly everywhere.

Nong, Oey, and Nachon set up the kitchen on the veranda of the public temple hall, a gorgeous hall, 150 x 75 feet, raised on hardwood pillars. I look at them in awe; you won't find trees like that anymore in Thailand. The floor is made of hardwood too. The floor boards differ in size, some are over three feet wide. For a person who grew up on a parquet floor with regular tiles bought from a builder's market, it is a dazzling sight.

Only the short sides of the hall have walls. There is a poster: No smoking, no drinking, no gambling. Next to it a sign with the names of the people who have donated money for building and maintaining the temple, with the amounts contributed next to the names. The ridge of the roof is thirty-five feet up. Buddha statues stand all around, with a throne with lots of gold and decorations in the centre. There is a table where monks put out the food they don't need themselves, everything wrapped in plastic. It is cool, it is quiet, it is the temple hall of my dreams. 'Sabai, Nong!' I say enthusiastically. But Nong doesn't think it's relaxed at all. 'Very big, cleaning big job! You cleaning!' and she shoves a broom into my hands. She is in stitches when I immediately get going on the floorboards, while she starts preparing dinner. She'll make *mieang kham*, my favourite. Green leaves with a mixture of roasted coconut, shallots, peanut, chilli, palm sugar, lime, and ginger. You fold the leaf and pop it into your mouth, and wham! An explosion of tastes, tears in your eyes, your throat gets scorched, your stomach braces itself . . . and when the tempest subsides, you feed in the next rocket round.

Early in the night, there is a loud cracking sound. Dok-ngeon has picked up the art of breaking trees from Si-nuan. She trumpets loudly when Wiset and Duang tie her to another tree. Every now and then, a dessicated teak leaf falls on my tent. Those leaves are so big and heavy it sounds as if a dead bird has dropped on the fabric. Every time the wind blows them about, I think a rain shower has started.

***

At six o'clock in the morning, the first motorbike is kick-started, followed right away by decibel waves from a riding sound system. The world nowadays is flooded with decibels, and Thailand is no exception.

Pa Kaeo is ill. He doesn't eat, he throws up, and doesn't respond when Mongkhon jumps on him. Doctor Nit comes by with her medicine box and jabs some needles in the skinny body. Yut gets a can of fish and mixes it with rice and curry sauce. Duang nods in approval: 'Pa Kaeo ma thai!' Pa Kaeo is a Thai dog! He doesn't think much of my puppy food efforts. Thai food will probably make the critter feel better. Pa Kaeo eats, but spits it out again. I carry him to my tent and put him next to me on the inflatable bed. He is weak and washed-out. If only he was still the Lopburi vandal. In Buddha's name, please don't let anything happen to Pa Kaeo.

In old Sukhothai, history and tourism rule. New Sukhothai is the place for shops, markets, offices, and houses. Yut takes us to the district headquarters in the mini-van. The meeting with three serious looking officials shows just how much our confidence has grown. Lee speaks for a quarter of an hour about our achievements in Ayutthaya and Lopburi, about Si-nuan and Dok-ngeon, about the Elephant Nature Park. He talks about our website: 'You could be mentioned on it as well!' The officials deliberate amongst themselves, with Lee and with Doctor Nit, and slowly our Sukhothai week takes shape. The locations for the school programme and the animal clinic are chosen. Tomorrow we can join the festivities in which Sukhothai commemorates Ramkhamhaeng, an ancient king whose name is inextricably linked with elephants. Of course, there will be elephants in a parade, and in the evening we can witness an enacted battle with elephants.

I ask if it would be possible for us to hold the animal clinic at the historic centre. Shocked, the officials shake their heads. 'The historic centre is connected with the King, we cannot allow people to take dogs and cats over there!' I bring up the baby elephant we saw at the market. Do they know where it is being hidden during the day? 'No, we try to send all begging elephants away, but they hide in different places. When we see one, can we call you?' Do they really think we are going to bring every elephant home? In that case our campaign is a little too successful. 'You would do better to call the animal office,' Lee says, and he shows them the documents a mahout has to carry when he's on the road with an elephant. 'How many elephants are there in Thailand?' one of the district chiefs asks. I am surprised. So much ignorance in a city with a splendid elephant history, with a festival where the national symbol plays a leading part. The historical elephant is better protected than the living one.

The animal office is our next stop—two computers, filing cabinets, and a lot of stamps. The officials have already been informed about our arrival, thanks to faxes from the national headquarters, and they are very accommodating. Doctors will come and help spay and neuter, just like last week in Lopburi.

Seven hundred years ago, Ramkhamhaeng, still a prince at nineteen, then later the third king of the Sukhothai dynasty, climbed on his elephant and defeated his Mon challenger in single combat. Once mounted to the throne, he managed to expand Sukhothai in all directions. Ramkhamhaeng wasn't just a great warrior, he was also a benevolent ruler, judging by an ancient stone inscription: *'Under King Ramkhamhaeng life in Sukhothai is good. There are fish in the water, and rice in the fields. The King doesn't demand taxes of those who travel the roads, or those who wish to sell their oxen and horses. Who wants to trade horses can do so. The people are happy.'* Not a bad spin-doctor's spiel, back in the thirteenth century.

Ramkhamhaeng was also a spiritual leader. He invented the Thai alphabet, invited monks to teach the people of Sukhothai the lessons of Buddha, and had many temples built. Both in doctrine and in architecture, he focused on the Buddhism of Sri Lanka (Ceylon), to show that the Khom (ancient Cambodian people) were part of Sukhothai history. That's why, besides the 'corn cob towers', there are pagodas that remind one of India, bell-shaped with a slim, pointed spire on top. Just as in Ayutthaya and Lopburi, the historical park here is a wonderful place to wander around in. Of the many *wihan*, the Buddhist prayer halls, only the pillars remain, straight and crooked, half and whole. Together with their shadows, they produce beautiful, rhythmic patterns.

The most beautiful temple of them all is a little outside the park walls. Wat Si Chum was built around a huge statue of Buddha. Just the hand, curled loosely over the knee of Buddha seated in the lotus posture, is more than man-sized. Phra Achana is his name: the Fearless One. The statue is closely enfolded within the walls of the roofless temple. This is the site where they found the stone inscription which proclaims the happiness of the people of Sukhothai in the reign of Ramkhamhaeng.

On the seventeenth of January every year, the city commemorates its hero with a festival at the historical park. It starts in the morning below the statue of Ramkhamhaeng, depicted as a beautiful man, with the same sensual lips that adorn so many statues of Buddha. After secular speeches and religious chants, a band of classical Thai instruments accompanies groups of dancers. Gracefully and subtly, they weave their patterns of motion on the scorching hot plateau at the feet of Ramkhamhaeng. 'Their head dresses are straight from the museum,' Lee tells me. 'They are lent out for this day.' Modern Thai pop music envelopes the entrance of the park, where booths with merchandise represent the money part of the festival. Old and new forming a perfect match once again.

***

At ten o'clock we get a phone call: the doctors from the animal office are at Wat Ban Na, bursting with zeal to make their contributions to animal birth control. When we arrive, their long table is already set up in the main temple hall, and the first dog is knocked-out. There is a smell of disinfectant, and a long line has formed at the table where Oey is registering patients' owners. Doctor Nit waves her needles energetically. There are four television crews, one local and three national, and a phone call comes in from the regional radio station that wants to do a live interview with Lee and me tomorrow. *Bring the elephant home* has become a well-oiled machine.

Halfway through the morning, Tul comes up to me and introduces himself. He is a young artist, working on a children's book about how mother animals take care of their babies. When he visited the Elephant Nature Park as a volunteer, Lek referred him to us. It is nice talking to him, especially since you don't meet too many young Thai who are worried about street elephants. 'People my age often only see the symbolic meaning of the elephant,' he says. 'They buy a statue that is supposed to bring good fortune, and that is it.' Tul grew up in the United States. Since he has been drawing animals from an early age, he spent a lot of time in zoos. 'But you only really see how animals experience the world around them when you live with them.' We agree there are actually two kinds of questions when it comes to wild animals. The first one is philosophical: should you domesticate them, should you lock them up in zoos? The other one is practical. When you have domesticated wild animals, how do you deal with them? 'The Elephant Nature Park is an answer to the second question,' I say. 'What did you think of it?' 'Very, very good. It is honest, it is about the animals. I was astonished to hear I was the only Thai to volunteer.'

After the last of the dogs and cats have been de-sexed, de-manged, and de-loused, Channel 11 wants an interview in the field, near the elephants. Good idea. It's a long walk, their current day-care centre is far from the temple. We trudge across fields of stubble, up one bank, down another, the sun is burning hot, but the camera crew doesn't flinch. Then we see two grey mounds in the distance. Wet and muddy the ladies come towards us. Duang is wet too, he has just taken a bath in the pool near which the elephants play and eat. 'This is paradise,' he says. 'Swimming, fishing, not a soul to bother us.' Elephant dung is everywhere, once again I notice how much it smells like horseshit. Not that bad, really.

The interview is very straightforward. 'How do you think to solve the elephant problem?' 'Not on my own, in any case,' I say. 'I can't buy all the street elephants, and the Elephant Nature Park isn't big enough to take them all in. I would like to work together with the animal offices. There should also be more space for the elephants to live in, both for the wild and the house elephants. We need to co-operate with the mahouts. There is not enough food in their villages for the elephants, they have to go out into the streets to be able to feed their families and elephants. They are in just as much trouble as the elephants.' Just listen to me. I have changed. Mahouts used to be the villains who exploited elephants and beat them up with their goads. Now they are Duang and Wiset and Narong, people who have been marginalised in the course of history. People without whom a solution is not possible.

I try to sell the TV-crew on the idea of doing a story on the baby elephant that is wandering about Sukhothai. 'If we find her, we could maybe work out a solution, together with the animal office.' They say they will think about it.

At the Internet cafe, I read my e-mails. A man from Canada has transferred two thousand euros for the purchase of a piece of land to expand the Elephant Nature Park. I am delighted. Including Dok-ngeon and Si-nuan, there are now twenty-nine elephants at the Park. It is full.

Pa Kaeo is still ill. His rug is surrounded by bowls with food and drink. Yut says he has spat out the fish he ate. Doctor Nit comes over with a drip. Isn't that a little overdone? She says Pa Kaeo is too young and too thin to survive if he doesn't ingest something. The needle of the drip looks like a drill. Pa Kaeo screams when it goes in, and screams even more when a large lump grows under his skin. 'Get that needle out! Stop!' I scream along with him. The needle comes out and I comfort Pa Kaeo. I used to be scared about needles when I had to take Moppie to the vet as a child.

We go back to old Sukhothai in the evening, to see the last part of the Ramkhamhaeng festival. A parade is moving into the historical park. Floats and groups in identical shirts. The low sun deepens the colours and makes the gold sparkle. But it is clear that Thai are not a marching people, even with the aid of a drum band nobody is keeping in step. The atmosphere is solemn, but nevertheless people in the parade are eating, drinking, and making calls on their cell phones. Up front are three elephants in full fighting outfit, tough looking men with long spears on their backs. At the rear a group of important men stride by, heading for the seats of honour in front of the main stage. 'There, that man in the green silk suit, the minister of labour!' Lee hisses. 'Go for it!' For the elephants I'll do anything. Boldly I jump into the group, greet the minister politely and present my business card. He listens kindly to my stammering attempt to explain *Bring the elephant home*. I don't know if he understood anything, but Lee is beaming. 'If I had done something like that, I would be on the ground by now, with two security people on top of me. A foreigner can get away with this!'

The show performed is like a Hollywood production. The ancient history of Ramkhamhaeng, his fight on an elephant, the peace in his kingdom, and the creation of the Thai alphabet are all accompanied by fire works and atmospheric light and sound effects. A deep, resonant voice tells the story, accompanied by a western-style musical score during which a large vividly costumed troupe performs traditional dances. A forest of fingers bending backwards, two hundred heads swaying to the left, inclining to the right.

The fight between the king and his enemy is spectacular. It involves three elephants, each with a warrior equipped with a long spear riding on its neck. Behind them, on howdahs, men are wielding swords. The elephants have giant tusks and look splendid in their red and gold covers. How fast they are, how nimble! At times they pass each other at full speed, then the warriors clang their spears together. The elephants are next positioned head to head and try to force each other back, as bulls do in the wild when fighting for dominance. The largest one even lifts his opponent off the ground, his tusks locked underneath its opponent's.

So this is what the Thai mean when they speak with respect about the elephant that saved Siam. It is impressive. But the training of the animals couldn't have been gentle, and the bangs and flashes of the fireworks are terrifying. I may have changed, but a good show is still no excuse for animal cruelty. These are the same contradictory feelings I try to express in the interview the next morning, in the studio of the regional radio station FM 99.25 Mhz. Unfortunately, I immediately catch a cold from the air-conditioning in the building, causing me to introduce myself as 'Adoidette van de Wader, founder ob Brink De Eleband Hobe.' The interviewer touches a raw spot by asking how I liked the elephant fight. 'I was impressed by its beauty,' I say diplomatically, 'but it may not have been so great for the elephants.' I talk about my reasons for wanting to improve the situation of the street elephants. 'Can you do something for the two-month-old baby that is on the streets in Sukhothai?' the interviewer asks. I repeat what I said on television the day before. Co-operation with the government, alternatives for the mahouts, expansion of habitat for the elephants. Lee is asked about the Thai public. What are we doing to make the Thai understand about what we are doing? Lee emphasises the importance of our school programme. Start young, he says. 'Children have to experience that elephants are beautiful and that you should love them.' 'And how will you get the government to listen?' Lee: 'Ever since Lek has become Hero of Asia, the Elephant Nature Park is getting a lot of positive attention. They know who we are now.' Our ambassador has found his form. He makes a passionate appeal to be kind to all animals. 'Don't abandon them, don't leave it to the temples to care for them. Do come and see our elephants, and visit our website. Doubleyou doubleyou doubleyou Bring the elephant home dot org.' The interviewer concludes: 'I hope that you will be successful soon, Miss Antoinette.'

During the interview, the president of the radio station has come in to take pictures. Now he warmly shakes our hands. 'Most Thai don't approve of elephants walking the streets. They give money because they love animals, although they know they are maintaining this begging. All foreigners who can contribute to solving the elephant problem are welcome. With our radio programmes, we want to support animal protection in this region.' He rummages in a large basket with food items, looking for a suitable present, then gives us the whole basket. 'Just mention my name to the president of the radio station in Chiang Mai, then they can report on your arrival at the Elephant Nature Park.'

On our way back to the camp, a mahout from Phuket calls. He claims to know where Nung Ning is. 'Never mind,' Lee says. In the evening we search the night market in new Sukhothai for the two-month-old baby elephant, in vain.

***

Day four starts with the animal clinic in a neighbouring temple. Everybody is a little anxious about the approaching arrival at the Park. Still, about fifty animals are treated. In the afternoon Si-nuan and Dok-ngeon go to school for the last time. It is close to the temple, we only have to walk thirty feet along the road to get there. When we cross the sports field, we can hear the children yelling. 'Chang ma laeo!' The elephants are coming! In the school's open-sided pavilion, we hang up our banner between portraits of Napoleon and Baden Powell. They would be surprised to know they are helping to promote our project.

Thanks to our having made a previous visit to the headmaster of the school, all three hundred children have brought elephant drawings, along with lots of sugar cane, bananas, and other elephant snacks. The teachers are firmly in charge, even when seated on the ground the children form perfectly straight lines. The *Chang* song is sung at typhoon strength, and no matter how often we have practised it, our Dutch song sounds like a whimper in comparison. 'I am a little elephant, I wander through the woods . . .' If only I were a little elephant, then I wouldn't have to sing for three hundred children and a teaching staff. Not to mention the viciously giggling Yut and Nong.

We are faced with a problem in the elephant quiz. Everybody on the same side of the rope? Embarrassed, the teachers look away. That is just not done, boys and girls together! Well, maybe just this once. The children don't know about embarrassment. Just as in Ayutthaya and in Lopburi, they jump around like foals, across the rope and back, but this time we can't even pick a winner because they all have the correct answers. They even know elephants can't jump.

The film crew of Nature Conservation Films, that filmed us extensively in November, catches up with us again. They say that Animal Planet, the station that had as good as promised to buy and show the documentary, thought the material too harsh. Too many sad elephants, too much cruelty. 'The people want pretty wildlife photography and happy elephants.' What a letdown. The world wants to be deceived. Now the crew will register our arrival, and will return later on to extensively film the happy elephants in the Park. Their life stories, their social ties, their communication. We discuss the programme for the next few days. 'Upon arrival in Mae Taeng, we'll unload the elephants about three miles before we reach the Park,' I say. 'We'll walk the last part, to keep some of the original idea alive. Tomorrow morning you can film our animal clinic in a neighbouring village, and I will try to arrange an elephant ceremony at Wat Chang Lom. *Lom* means 'to circle'. Wat Chang Lom is an ancient temple nearby. Around its base, thirty-six sculpted elephants keep guard. We can get there using a back-road. It is a magical place, very quiet, a little neglected. A ceremony in this place, with elephants and monks, at the end of the afternoon, that would be wonderful.

The last quiet evening. We use it for a team farewell ceremony. I thank everyone from the bottom of my heart, and pass out presents from Holland, and a bonus. We divvy up all of the cooking and camping gear. Yut and Nong give Hanna and me a wooden elephant with coasters on its back, Nachon and Oey have a sun hat for everyone. *Khit thueng* . . . I will miss them, all of them.

At breakfast, Lee already has his big book of numbers out, for one of our last *checkbins*. Apparently the expenses keep rising a little every day, by now they are sixty-five euros a day on average. That's normal, our team has grown all the time. 'Who are all these people?' Evert from the film crew asked in surprise when we gathered to eat one of Nong's five-star dinners, 'Are they all camping here?' 'All *Bring the elephant home* people', I told him proudly.

At the animal clinic in a village square, a hundred applicants are dealt with in two hours, a record. Between the barking dogs and hissing cats, an old blind man zigzags onto the square, calling out softly. No one pays any attention until Lee notices and escorts him to the temple where he can get a free meal. Ten points for Lee, once again.

In the afternoon, we hold open house in front of the temple. It is sweltering hot. We peg up three hundred children's drawings onto a clothesline, before mothers and fathers arrive with their potential prize winners on mopeds and motorbikes. Si-nuan and Dok-ngeon strip banana trees, the monks have their pictures taken with the elephants, the film crew's camera rolls. They ask if we can load the elephants onto the truck in front of the camera because tonight, when we take off for Mae Taeng, it'll be too dark. We call Nachon and the mahouts to walk the elephants to a hillock onto which the tailboard of the truck can be lowered, and then a terrible accident nearly happens. Dok-ngeon is in a bad mood, perhaps because of the commotion, perhaps the heat, who knows. While she is being ushered onto the truck, she turns around and almost crushes Wiset against its side. At the final moment, one of my nightmares almost comes true. 'I'll be glad to have my two daughters at the Park tomorrow', Lee says. I regret this action, since tomorrow the elephants will have a hard enough time as it is. For this reason, I decide to cancel the trip to Wat Chang Lom. Pity. But everyone is tired, and we need to regain our strength for tomorrow. The day I have worked for, over the past two years.

***

That night Pa Kaeo sleeps peacefully on my belly. He is doing better. My head is a merry-go-round. By this time tomorrow, it will be over. The elephants will be home, and I won't have any more responsibilities. Tomorrow night I will drink an unbelievable amount of Chang beer.

The alarm rings at four o'clock. The mahouts already have a fire going. At four thirty, the monks shine a spotlight on our teak grove, and start sweeping leaves. Their orange robes seem to drift between the tall, straight trunks like ghosts from times long gone. Fortunately, they are also smoking and hawking, which shakes me from my surreal state of mind. I roll up the sleeping bag, fold the tent, load up.

This time, both ladies step into the truck like lambs. It is still cold, the mahouts make a charcoal fire in a terracotta stove in the back of the truck to keep warm. At five twenty-five, Nachon turns on the ignition and we're off on the final two hundred miles. Lee folds his hands, closes his eyes, and meditates.

At seven thirty we stop, engine running, at a checkpoint for transportation papers. Thumping in the back, oh yes, elephants. I still haven't completely reconnected with reality. The film crew pops up on fly-overs every once in a while. From these high angles, they can get good shots of the transport. At nine thirty, Lee gets a call. Unfortunately, the officials of the animal office of Chiang Mai won't be present when we arrive, they all had to go to the airport to welcome a minister. But Channel 7, a local television station, will be there.

When we approach Chiang Mai, Si-nuan loses it. She hammers her tusk on Dok-ngeon's forehead, and as small as that bit of ivory is, she still makes a large gash. I take the first-aid kit and climb onto the cabin roof to help Wiset. Using three packs of cottonwool, we disinfect the wound. Dok-ngeon is bleeding like crazy. That will be a pretty sight on TV. Just a little bit longer girls, hang on.

Lee and I sit nervously next to each other in the truck. Every fifteen minutes we go over our plan, road map on our lap. Our phones keep ringing. Lek calls: at what time will we arrive exactly? What? Four o'clock? Far too late, the sun sets early, and a Korean camera crew is waiting. Hurry up! Pom calls to say she and a group of volunteers are waiting at the side of the road. A reporter from a city newspaper calls about directions. Doctor Nit calls to say she is stuck in Chiang Mai and won't be there in time. I don't care any more. We're almost there.

When we drive into Mae Taeng, we pass a group of elephants from a trekking camp. There's even a baby elephant. At least our elephants are on their way to freedom, I think hazily. I spot a group of volunteers waving. Mahouts from the Park run alongside the truck to point out the best spot to unload. There are several film cameras. Lek hugs me: 'You made it!' From Mae Taeng on, we walk through the woods, on a path where passing cars and mopeds throw up dust clouds. Narong rides Si-nuan, Wiset walks next to Dok-ngeon, Duang follows them. Lek has made a walk-by buffet along the path, with pineapples, bananas, and melons laid out nicely on banana leaves. Si-nuan digs into the fruit, Dok-ngeon is more interested in the forest greens along the path. 'A real jungle girl,' Lek teaches the volunteers. 'When she has a choice, she prefers jungle food. She has been captured in the wild and has not yet been with people for long, you can tell.'

Duang's calloused forefinger points out all sorts of trees along the path. 'Elephants can eat that one, and that one, and that one too.' And when we pass the banana plantation bought with the money from *Bring the elephant home*, he says: '*Di mak!* Very good! If this is for the elephants, I wouldn't mind being an elephant here.'

Then we leave the dusty path and walk towards the river. Si-nuan and Dok-ngeon drink and spray themselves with water. Now we are really travelling through elephant country. This is what I've always had in mind. It is wonderful to see how Si-nuan begins to remember her roots. When we come across elephant dung, she sniffs it, flaps her ears, and keeps sounding that deep, otherworldly rumble elephants use to communicate. Where are you? I know you're around! In all this time we've been together, I have never heard that sound even once. It is almost as if life is flowing back into her. Dok-ngeon is quiet, she walks after Si-nuan, and eats and eats.

Then we can remove the chains. We stand all around the elephants and cheer, Dok-ngeon trumpets with us. Lee and I do a high five together: 'Mission completed!' Together we walk through the gate of the Elephant Nature Park.

✳✳✳

Lek has urged all the volunteers and visitors onto the veranda of the central hut, from where they are welcoming us. A monk is there, too, with bowl of sanctified water and a twig. When we get closer, he tries to bless the newcomers, but most of the benediction sprinkles the other elephants crowding around the hut in anticipation of the feast. My eyes fill with tears when I see Si-nuan and Dok-ngeon amongst all my old loves, but this is not yet the time for an emotional outburst. First, I need to talk to the press, and answer questions from the people at the Park. I see Narong and another mahout put their arms around each others shoulders and take off for their huts. Duang keeps a bit to the side. I see him watching all the fuss and hear him mumble something about *farang*, foreigners. Pa Kaeo sits on the lap of one of the volunteers. People with cameras and microphone booms are everywhere. Bedlam! I am walking around just as dazed as Dok-ngeon, who wants nothing to do with all the fuss, and walks off into the field on her own. Si-nuan, on the other hand, feels like a fish in water. Her trunk curls eagerly around one of the baby elephants, she walks here, marches there, and then discovers Hope, a little down the field. Hey, what a funny boy! When she approaches him, Hope stretches out his trunk, straight at her. Come on, if you dare! A game of push and pull develops, they fool around for at least an hour. Hope alternately offers his front and his back end. His front end seems to appeal to Si-nuan. Trunks curl around each other, are put in ears and mouths. Apparently, Hope's back end is not as alluring. Every time he pushes his behind against her trunk, she whacks him. 'Hope is making a few mistakes in his approach,' Lek says.

In the meantime, Duang and his wife have looked up Malai Thong, their old elephant Lek bought in Surin. Duang wants to check on her leg, the leg with which she stepped on a mine. He gets her on her knees with a few words. He inspects the wound and calls Doctor Nit. She takes her medical bag, and Duang gives the injection himself. 'What is that?' an American visitor asks appalled. 'Disinfectant,' the imperturbable Doctor Nit says.

At the end of the afternoon, the troop of elephants moves to the river for a bath. Si-nuan and Dok-ngeon go with them as if they have been members of the team for years. Suddenly, Lilly appears next to Si-nuan. On the road, I daydreamed about them becoming friends, is it going to happen? But the mutual sniffing each other out turns into pushing, and then all of a sudden the shit hits the fan. They spread their ears, butt their foreheads against each other, and their front legs even leave the ground as they trumpet war cries and I wonder what would have happened if Narong hadn't jumped in to pull Si-nuan out by her ear. Such violence, and from these elderly ladies! So much for friendship.

The number of visitors has gone up again. At dinner, the lines have doubled in front of the tables with the food. 'The Park is such a great place for the children,' I hear a Danish mum say. A vegan Englishman tells his neighbour that the Internet is a great help in ethical consuming. And an oh-my-god-American woman shows off the silk trousers she has bought at the shop. The Park has found its public. Too bad there aren't more Thai visitors.

I get congratulations and questions from all sides. It is good to see Pom and Lek again, and Michelle, Karl, Jody, James, and Chom, the mahouts Luang, Dichai, and Bochu, and all the other veterans, but only half of me is present. I walk around in a daze, I feel weightless. The burden has been lifted from my shoulders, and the Chang beer does the rest. It is over, it is over. Later, I drop off into a dreamless sleep. I wake up to the familiar sounds of trumpeting, rumbling, and grazing. In the morning sun, I walk to the central hut, and come across a scene that would beat the Sukhothai elephant fight any day. Si-nuan gets a family.

Early in January, a mother with a six-day-old baby elephant was brought to the Park. Mae Tokoh, the mother, worked at a trekking camp and had been forced to carry on with this until the day of birth. The baby—'Pupia', Wiset says, when I ask about his name—was unable to grow to full size in its mother's womb due to the tight howdah girth. After arriving at the Park, it looked as if Pupia wasn't going to make it. He was given additional bottle-feeding, and was watched closely. Now, three weeks later, he walks around cheerfully, with Malai Thong as a guardian aunt. Mother, son, and aunt form a close-knit trio.

Yesterday, Si-nuan made the baby's acquaintance, today she is seriously applying for the job of second aunt. It is a breathtaking and touching spectacle. The three big elephants orbit each other, their heads stay close all the time, sometimes they seem to be one huge, three-headed body. They push, they turn, they steam. Their trunks purposefully find each other's body openings, ears, mouths, tear glands. The strangest noises emanate from this slowly turning grey mass. Rumbling, blowing, growling, squeaking, purring, sucking, and when a trunk hits the ground with a dry tap, you can hear how hollow this tube really is, and how big the resonating forehead. Meanwhile, Pupia lurches between the twelve slow-moving ladies' legs. He is especially curious about Si-nuan. He looks for her nipples, tries to get milk from her breasts, licks her genitals, and wriggles his tiny trunk into her large trunk. Si-nuan's hormones are waking up, she is constantly urinating, and seeks out the baby with her trunk. This is going well. The Thai government should see this, I think, no, the whole of Thailand, the whole of Asia, the entire world, then there would be no more elephants on the streets, then we would respect the forest and allow the animals their share of the world.

The family members take their midday bath together. When Pupia falls, a trunk immediately appears to pull him out of the water. Dok-ngeon is hesitantly paddling. I splash water on her, she slips into the water sideways and sits down on her behind to enjoy herself. I immerse myself, too, and float along with the fast-flowing river. 'I am a little elephant, I wander through the woods, usually I wear a leash, today I can go free! O yes, o yes, o yes, o yes, o yeeeeeeeees!'

Epilogue

THE ONLY TEAM member for whom I am still responsible at this stage is Pa Kaeo, and I have to make a decision. Take him to Amsterdam, get a doggy stairway to my skylight and a carrier bicycle? 'Pa Kaeo would be cold in Holland,' Lee mutters. After a long hesitation, I leave him with Lee's father, where he can be outside throughout the day. When I look up, he is running around the house with another dog. He is not very interested in me. Pa Kaeo is becoming a real Thai dog.

And then I am alone again in Thailand. I have kept my promise, the supporters don't expect anything from me for a while. At first I feel a little uprooted and aimless, but then I find room to breathe, to think about the future.

I have three months left in Thailand, and decide to talk to people here who dedicate themselves to improving the lives of street elephants. Perhaps I should have done this a lot sooner. On the other hand, I am glad I didn't, because the elephant groups appear to be divided between themselves about which strategy to follow. They have tried a lot, and a lot has failed. If I'd talked to them beforehand, I might never have undertaken anything at all.

As a reporter, Pittaya Homkrailas wrote a story about elephants in 1988 and became so fascinated with them that he has devoted his life to their protection. He worked in Surin province for ten years, and researched the ancient elephant culture in the villages. In 1994, he was co-founder of the Thai Foundation of Elephant Lovers. To Pittaya, protecting elephants means protecting mahouts and their ancient culture. He was sad to see the begging in cities, but when the law against it came into effect in 2003 and the mahouts were driven out of Bangkok, Pittaya was on their side. He was there when the desperate mahouts assembled in Surin and decided to take action. He participated in the elephant protest march, from Surin to Bangkok. The government then allocated quite a bit of money to moving the street elephants and their mahouts to a nature reserve, where they were supposed to work as park rangers. This was one of the failed projects. 'There was no organisation, no supervision,' Pittaya says.

He himself tried to set up a mahout homestay programme in Surin. 'Arresting mahouts in the city and sending them home is not a solution,' he says. 'They have no work and no food there. We need to develop a new way of life for man and elephant in their own villages, and we can't do that without tourism.' But his programme failed as well, according to him because of poor marketing. The travel agency involved didn't send any guests.

I travel to Pattaya, the beach resort south of Bangkok, where there is a mahout homestay programme set up by Eco Volunteers Tours. Previously, the programme was in Ban Tha Klang, in Surin, where it failed. 'The mahouts didn't feel involved,' the manager says. 'They would be drinking whiskey in the morning, and didn't want any meddlesome volunteers around. Here it works. The mahouts provide elephant trips for tourists, the volunteers do chores around the camp.'

That is not quite what I had in mind. 'The forest belongs to the elephants,' a girl in Lopburi wrote on the drawing she made for our school programme, and she was right. Elephants should live in the forest, not be chained up until they can go for another trip along the beach carrying tourists.

Richard Lair is the president of the Elephant Conservation Centre in Lampang, a centre supported by the government where elephants and mahouts go for training. He came from the US to Asia in the 1970s, 'hoping to be overwhelmed by a primeval world,' as he writes in his book *Gone Astray*. 'But instead I became the unhappy witness of an incessant and irreversible depreciation of the skills, knowledge, and ethos needed for good elephant care.'

At the Elephant Conservation Centre mahouts and elephants perform in a show in which they demonstrate the workings of the logging industry in earlier days. You can go for a ride. The centre is also proud of its elephants that paint and make music. Lair himself directs the elephant orchestra. The centre also functions as a shelter for 'arrested' street elephants. After things have been arranged with the mahout in question, the elephant is sent back in a truck. Not a very enjoyable course of action for any of the parties involved. The elephant is shuttled about like a piece of cargo, the mahout loses a lot of money and begins to hate the centre. Lair believes all the street elephants should be employed in trekking camps and shows. 'They have to get away from Isan,' he says, 'it has no tourism, and tourism is the elephants' only chance of survival. Giving elephants back their natural habitat? 'Nice plan, but how are the mahouts going to make a living?'

Roger Lohanan, of the Thai Society of Animal Protectors has been committed to getting elephants off the street for years. He is the man who frightened me earlier on, with his threats to put an end to the walk. It took till now for us to come together to sit down and talk. He says his organisation's extensive investigation into street elephants was instrumental in the passage of the law against using elephants for begging. He focuses on the animals. 'I have no respect for traditions if they involve cruelty against animals.' He calls mahouts cowboys, Mafia, businessmen, and in return they don't feel a lot of love for him.

Roger believes the elephants in Surin could benefit from a workplace where they could all go. A kind of elephant festival, but throughout the year. The government should assume responsibility in this. Roger approves of the mahout salary, provided the mahout gets every bit of the promised eight thousand baht. 'Some outside parties should be involved in checking on the process. That might be a good start for you,' he says. 'Listen to the mahouts, make sure the money gets to them, and let their voices be heard.' He would love to work together with me, and has no problem with me as a westerner, just doing the things I care about. His objections to *Bring the elephant home* were purely focused on the planned walk, not about me personally, he says. From the moment the walk had been cancelled, he considered his job done. He even thinks our educational programme is excellent, and even his own organisation could learn from it.

Roger thinks that within five years there will be no more wild elephants in Thailand. 'Therefore, we have to make sure that the domesticated ones can survive under good conditions. We mainly engage in protective legislation and practical measures, like the presence of vets at trekking camps and elephant shows. And when elephants can get a better life abroad, I am not opposed to exporting them.' He is the only Thai I have ever met who thinks like this. When it comes to exporting elephants, people generally bristle with outrage.

Soraida Salwala is founder and president of Friends of the Asian Elephant (FAE). She too criticised our *Bring the elephant home* project at first but, just like Roger Lohanan, she has changed her mind. Now she thanks me for my efforts. Soraida's love for elephants is rooted in her childhood, as is Lek's. When she was eight years old, she saw an elephant lying by the side of the road, hit by a truck. 'We must take it to the hospital,' she cried to her father. But there was none. Elephant hospitals have become one of the main activities of FAE. The organisation also engages in lobbying and advising the government, and holds demonstrations. For example, in 2006 Soraida and her allies blocked the road for an elephant transport, destination Australia. The FAE has also dedicated itself to banning street elephants in Bangkok and other cities. Soraida deplores the fact that no other means of existence has been provided for the mahouts, a measure the FAE had asked for. Illegal trade and poaching occur every day, she says, and business people and politicians are involved. The government should use its authority to intervene, and protect the elephants and their habitat. There should be laws, and the means to uphold them. A permanent elephant centre should be created in Ban Tha Klang, with potential for tourism, and public land where food for the elephants can be grown.

The people I talk to seem to agree on many issues. There should be more stringent protection laws for elephants, and the law should be upheld more strictly. The word tourism is always mentioned, as is conservation of habitat. The traditional elephant culture is seen by most as valuable, and I get the impression that everybody would be pleased to see it preserved. Everybody also believes you can't just leave the mahouts without a means of support, even though different solutions are suggested. But why then, is this front so divided? Maybe it's because the organisations have to compete with each other for funding, or maybe people are a lot like bull elephants that can't put up with each other very well.

The discussions taught me a lot, but a clear strategy for the future still eludes me. Regrettably, because the number of street elephants is noticeably growing. Every time I visit Bangkok, I see more of them caught up in traffic jams, begging at markets, and waiting outside the exits of crowded bars.

One night around two o'clock, I am sitting in front of a snackbar in the city centre. Every night, a five-year-old elephant takes its stand here. I watch the world swirling around her. A westerner passes, involved in heated negotiations with a Thai. He sees the elephant and yells: 'What the fuck is this?' The Thai man distracts him, and they disappear into the crowd. A young Thai woman hunches a shoulder to squeeze a cell phone against her ear and takes notes on her palm top computer at the same time. When a trunk is about to take the computer from her hand, she pulls a hundred baht from her pocket, gives it to the mahout, receives a bag of bananas, and feeds it to the elephant, while she is still on the phone and holding the palm top computer in her outstretched hand away from the trunk. A noisy, fat Western man, with a giggling Thai girlfriend on his arm, gives money to the mahout, the girlfriend feeds the bananas. A group of Thai boys in kilts and carrying bag pipes are oblivious to the elephant that is restlessly swaying back and forth.

I have to continue.

But how?

Take every street elephant to the Elephant Nature Park, that's what I will fight for, in any case. Because after everything I have seen and heard, one conclusion stands out: in the Elephant Nature Park domesticated elephants will live best. The north of Thailand is still real elephant country, even though it is being nibbled into from all sides. Lek says she will never stop buying land and elephants, while her ultimate goal is to free all elephants. For that I want to attract supporters, of course! But I also believe something should and could be done in other areas, especially in Surin. By combining reforestation, mahout salaries, and ecotourism, it should be possible to bring the elephants back home there as well. But Surin is an enormously complex challenge, that much I have figured out. I am not as naive as I used to be. The province presents a spectacle of elephant traders, corruption, violent training, conflicts of interests, and power games. But it would be wonderful if a project could be successful, there in the ancient elephant land.

The Thai activists I meet at demonstrations in the spring of 2006 tell me that I need a Thai organisation to work out plans to campaign on issues like these, and should start at the bottom. What do the mahouts themselves want? How can they recover their voice and speak out about their lives? We come up with schemes to put into motion. A massive petition with the participation of all the animal organisations, involve schools, the media, famous Thai, and of course a benefit festival in Bangkok, for which Chang Beer would be the obvious sponsor. I would like to do a school programme as well, after the good results on tour. With national art competitions where real artists would teach, an interactive website where schools can show their best drawings, an exhibition, and an auction. Bus loads of children going to the Elephant Nature Park.

I haven't figured it all out yet. But I am not done with Thailand, that's for sure. The experiences of the past two years have convinced me that you have to take action if you really want to change something. That you can make a difference, no matter how small. I want to spend my energy in matters I totally believe in and that make me happy. Life is too short for trivialities. But I have also learned to take the time for the small and beautiful things in life. I have learned that humour is important, that you can trust karma, and that you always have to make friends first.

After this experience I couldn't live in the Netherlands anymore. I couldn't stop thinking about the elephants, was missing Thailand like crazy. It didn't take long for me to decide to move to Thailand. We had to start new fundraising campaigns to keep supporting the elephants. For Dok-ngeon and Si-nuan we launched an adoption program. To expand their habitat and feed them and the other elephants in the Park, we bought a banana plantation and a new piece of land nearby. I tried to convince Dutch travel companies to include the Elephant Nature Park in their programmes instead of just offering a ride on the back of an elephant. Three of them did so far. We also began organising our own Chang tours: a holiday of three weeks in which participants can learn about elephants and experience the beauty of this country. They visit Elephant Nature Park, Elephant Conservation Centre, Elephant Dung Paper Project, and Boon Lott Elephant Sanctuary. They stay at the house of a mahout in Isan, hike in Khao Yai, learn about wild elephants, visit elephant temples, an elephant graveyard, and lots more. All profits go to . . . elephants! The Chang tours prove that elephant-friendly tourism is possible, and they support Thai elephant projects.

Today Si-nuan and Dok-ngeon are enjoying a happy life at the Elephant Nature Park, where they can spend the rest of their life as free elephants. Si-nuan has become a protecting auntie for baby Thong Kam, and stays near him all the time. She seems very happy with the little one near her, after she lost her own baby. She also takes care of Dok-ngeon with whom she became friends during their journey to the Elephant Nature Park. After arrival, Dok-ngeon was scared of all the elephants and people, but Si-nuan made sure she felt safe and introduced her to her own new family and friends. For Dok-ngeon it took almost half a year before she could enjoy being a young elephant. When I saw her playing in the mud bath with the baby elephants for the first time, my heart was full of joy. One job done!

'Return to the Wild', the documentary by Nature Conservation Films about our project, has been broadcast worldwide by Animal Planet, including in Thailand. It won two Roscar Awards, for 'best conservation documentary' and for 'most urgent appeal for action'. When we rescued baby elephant Faa Sai from training and street begging in November 2007, a Dutch TV channel reported about this in another documentary. Through these and similar initiatives, people have become more aware of the plight of street elephants, and more people visit animal-friendly parks such as the Elephant Nature Park. But we still have a lot of work to do.

The more I learned about elephants, the more I became aware that deforestation is the cause of many problems elephants are facing. Without trees, no elephants. To help all elephants in Thailand, we decided to tackle this issue and launched a new project for 2008: 'Trees for Elephants'. Within one year, we aimed to plant 100,000 trees, in areas where elephants are most in need. The project won the World of Difference Award of Vodafone, which provided me with a one-year salary and paid for all my personal expenses. By the end of August 2008, exactly one year later, the 100,000 trees were planted in several locations that are important for the protection of wild and domesticated elephants.

In and around the Elephant Nature Park, volunteers are constantly planting trees for elephants. At the Salakpra Wildlife Sanctuary and the Khao Yai National Park it is all about wild elephants. At Khao Yai, a corridor of trees will connect two forests, to expand the habitat of the wild elephants, and reduce conflict between people and elephants. In Salakpra Wildlife Sanctuary, slash and burn practices have seriously reduced the biological diversity of the forest, which consists of eighty percent bamboo today. Because of the lack of diversity, the animals disappear as well. The forest deteriorates and the elephants go and visit the plantations to find food. To restore plant diversity, we began a tree nursery and planted twenty-five different tree species.

In the next few years, we will continue with the tree projects. In Isan, we are cooperating with the Thai organisation Population and Community Development Association (PDA). Families in several villages will be helped to earn an income through a village development programme. For each tree the villagers plant, *Bring the elephant home* deposits twenty baht in a village bank where villagers can apply for a microcredit loan. Part of the profit of the village bank goes to the elephants as well. On an island in the river near the village of Ban Pai Noi, we are already creating an elephant island. We have planted the first 30,000 trees and by the end of the year, two street begging elephants can return home. To generate income with their elephants, the mahouts are starting different activities: a mahout homestay project so that visitors can stay with a traditional elephant family and get to know their culture, as well as learn how elephant dung paper and fertilizer are produced.

With the tree project along with four Thai partner organisations, *Bring the elephant home* has made a big step forward in improving the habitat and food problems of wild and domesticated elephants in Thailand. Planting the 100,000th tree was an incredible moment, as well as a great incentive to plant many more trees in the years to come. It has been a wonderful start, but we still have a long way to go to secure the future of Thai elephants.

To be continued!

For those who want to know what will happen next contact:
www.bring-the-elephant-home.org.

Afterword

E VEN THOUGH THIS book is written in the first person, it is a result of the collaboration of two authors. Antoinette van de Water is, as the book describes, initiator and driving force of *Bring the elephant home*. She wrote about her experiences on the project's website and in diaries. Liesbeth Sluiter witnessed parts of the adventure, from *Elephantasia* in Amsterdam to meeting Si-nuan and Dok-ngeon, and the trip from Surin to the Elephant Nature Park in Thailand. With Antoinette's website and diary reports and her own experiences, she composed the book before you.

Without the generous help from many people, we could never have brought Si-nuan and Dok-ngeon home, and this book would not have existed. We thank all our friends, supporters, volunteers, and sponsors of *Bring the elephant home*, the crew of *Elephantasia*, and the team of the Elephant Nature Park. We want to name in particular Sangduen Chailert (Lek), Jittra Chakan (Pom), Viritphon Chaiwong (Lee), the mahouts Narong, Duang and Wiset, Yut and Nong, Doctor Nit, Nachon and Oey, Anjana Suvarnananda (Tang), Sulaiporn Chonwilai (Noom), Roger Lohanan, Soraida Salwala, Pittaya Homkrailas, Richard Lair, Pieter J. Th. Marres of the Dutch embassy, Rob Faber, Rob Spaargaren, Hanna Jongepier, Eric Seuren, Berrie Jurg, Veronique Huijbregts, the Theresia School, Christien van Beek, Marjo Hoedenmaker, the Rentware company, the Vereniging Proefdiervrij, Joy Carolus, and Janette Symons.

Bibliography

Corvanich, Dr. Amnuay, and Michael Map-Joseph S. Thanyawongse. *Thai Elephant*. Forest Industry Organisation, 1999.

Gröning, Karl, and Martin Saller. *De olifant in de natuur en de cultuurgeschiedenis*. Könemann, 1999.

Lair, Richard. *The Elephant in Thai Life*. Asia Books, 2003.

——————. *Gone Astray. The Care and Management of the Asian Elephant in Domesticity*. Forest Industry Organisation and Food and Agricultural Organisation of the United Nations, Regional Office Asia and the Pacific, 1997.

Ping Amranand, and William Warren. *The Elephant in Thai Life and Legend*. Monsoon Editions, 1998.

Pittaya Homkrailas. *Ta Klang: The Elephant Valley of Mool River Basin*. Tourism Authority of Thailand, 2002.

Preecha Phuangkum, Richard Lair, and Taweepoke Angkawanith. *Elephant Care Manual for Mahouts and Camp Managers*. Forest Industry Organisation and Food and Agricultural Organisation of the United Nations, Regional Office Asia and the Pacific, 2005.

Shand, Mark. *India per olifant*. BZZTôH, 2002.

Interviews

Richard Lair, Lampang, March 16, 2006

Pittaya Homkrailas, Bangkok, March 22, 2006

Eco Volunteers, Pattaya, March 27, 2006

Roger Lohanan, Bangkok, April 19, 2006

Soraida Salwala, e-mail correspondence, May 1, 2006

Support Bring the Elephant Home

A ROUND 1900, THERE were at least 100,000 elephants in Thailand. Today there are about 2,000–3,000 domesticated and 1,500 wild animals. The domesticated population hardly reproduces, while the wild population is threatened by poaching and loss of habitat. The wild Thai elephant is an endangered species, and officially protected.

In the Thai tourist industry, elephants are big business. Business people buy elephants to hire them out to unemployed mahouts. The elephants are often overworked, poorly fed, ill-treated, and even drugged. The animals now live in the most crowded tourist areas, and sleep in parks or underneath motorway fly-overs. They risk getting hit by traffic, falling into holes, or stepping on sharp objects. The grass they eat is poisonous from the exhaust fumes, and there is not enough shade. To keep up with this hard work, they are given amphetamines. Family ties are virtually non-existent among these elephants. Babies are taken from their mothers too early to make training easier and more profitable.

Bring the elephant home shows there are natural, animal-friendly, and fun alternatives to get acquainted with elephants. We aim to support other initiatives like the Elephant Nature Park. By means of education, collaborating with elephant protection organisations, participating in direct action campaigns, and demanding better legislation, *Bring the elephant home* is fighting to get every elephant off the streets. In 2008 we planted 100,000 trees for elephants and we are now planning 'Trees for Elephants 2009.'

We cannot do this without supporters. Please help us to realise this project.

Send your donation to Bank Account number 1675200, Bring the Elephant Home, Vlaardingen, the Netherlands, IBAN: NL28 PSTB 0001 675200, BIC: PSTBNL21. Or donate online through: www.bring-the-elephant-home.org. Thank you so much!

Adopt an elephant!

☐ Yes, I would like to adopt Si-nuan / Dok-ngeon for 60 euro a year. I will transfer this amount to *Bring the elephant home*.

Name:
Address:

Town:
Postal code:
Country:
E-mail:

☐ I would like to receive the e-mail newsletter and updates about my foster elephants by e-mail.

Date:........./........./.........Signature:...

Bring the Elephant Home
Van Blankenheimstraat 36
3132 VB Vlaardingen
Tel 00 31 010 4600651
Fax 00 31 010 2342750
www.bring-the-elephant-home.org.
Antoinette@bring-the-elephant-home.nl
Chamber of Commerce, the Netherlands: 34216018
Postbank account number: 1675200

What to do when you see a street elephant in Thailand?

BUYING FOOD FOR the elephant will only perpetuate the problem. Elephants on the street are illegal. Call the National Park, Wildlife and Plant Conservation Department in Bangkok at 1362 (hotline) to report it, or contact an on-duty police officer in the vicinity.

Visit the Elephant Nature Park:

Do you want to give Dok-ngeon and Si-nuan bananas yourself, or scrub them down in the river? Do you want to experience Elephant Haven yourself? At www.elephantnaturefoundation.org you will find information on how to visit the Park, and apply as a volunteer.

Buy a Chang tour:

Bring the elephant home organises adventurous, animal-friendly trips where the elephant is at the centre of attention, and in which you get to see more of Thailand than just the beaches. For more information, contact: Antoinette@bring-the-elephant-home.nl.

Sponsor 'Trees for Elephants':

Without trees elephants don't have a chance to survive. Help create living space and food for Thai elephants. You can do this by making a donation to our project 'Trees for Elephants' at www.bring-the-elephant-home.org.